T0354102

# SERIAL MONOGAMY

## JOHN P. ROACH JR.

authorHOUSE®

AuthorHouse™
1663 Liberty Drive
Bloomington, IN 47403
www.authorhouse.com
Phone: 1-800-839-8640

First published by AuthorHouse 10/12/2011

ISBN: 978-1-4634-7449-2 (sc)
ISBN: 978-1-4634-7447-8 (e)
ISBN: 978-1-4634-7448-5 (dj)

Library of Congress Control Number: 2011915748


Printed in the United States of America

This book is printed on acid-free paper.

*Art and Architecture by John Patrick Roach Jr.*

# PREFACE

What is the purpose of Life?

While working for Corporate America, Kent finds the answer and lives by a code that he has defined for himself for success, happiness and love.

This is a true story taking place in Vermont and California. All names have been changed to protect the privacy of individuals.

An adaptation of the Award Winning Screenplay of the same title.

# Works of *John P. Roach Jr.*

**Historical Novels**
Mt. Soledad Love Story (Aristotle and Thomas Aquinas)
CALIFORNIA, The First 100 Years (Padre Serra to the Golden Spike)

**Biographical Novels**
The Fourteenth State (Ethan Allen)
Triumph of the Swan (Richard Wagner and King Ludwig II of Bavaria)
Absinthe (Edgar Degas, A Leader in the Impressionist Revolution)
The Mighty Kuchka (Nikolai Rimsky-Korsakov and The Russian Five.)

**Inspirational Books**
Serial Monogamy (A quest for finding Success, Happiness and Love)
Around the World in a Wheelchair (a motivational book for the
    disabled)
Thanks for the Memories Cookbook ( Deborah J. Johnson and Friends)

**Travel**
Experience America's Finest City on the San Diego Trolley

**Science Fiction**
Inquiring Minds (Teens challenge education system)

**Biographical Screenplays**
The Swan (Opera composer Richard Wagner and King Ludwig II)
Degas (Edgar Degas and the Impressionist Revolution in Art)
The Russian Five (Nikolai Rimsky-Korsakov and the Russian Five)
Vermont (Ethan Allen and the Green Mountain Boys.)
Mt. Soledad Love Story (Film version available to producers)
Serial Monogamy (An Award Winning Screenplay.)

**WEBSITE**
www.JPRoach.org

# DEDICATION

This book is dedicated to Darla, Carol, Kim, Lisa, Mary, Susan and Natalie.

# Table of Contents

| | | |
|---|---|---|
| I. | THE PURPOSE OF LIFE | 1 |
| II. | 1970 CORPORATE AMERICA | 5 |
| III. | VERMONT | 9 |
| IV. | FASCINATION | 11 |
| V. | INTERLUDE | 17 |
| VI. | THE SECRETARY | 21 |
| VII. | SUGARBUSH | 27 |
| VIII. | INSUBORDINATION | 31 |
| IX. | COMMITMENT | 33 |
| X. | MOTHERHOOD | 41 |
| XI. | THE SHRINK | 47 |
| XII. | ART | 51 |
| XIII. | ARCHITECTURE | 57 |
| XIV. | THE CURE | 59 |
| XV. | SERIAL MONOGAMY | 61 |
| XVI. | EUROPE | 69 |
| XVII. | SAILING | 73 |
| XVIII. | THE BALLERINA | 77 |
| XIX. | TORTOLA | 83 |
| XX. | MONTREAL | 89 |
| XXI. | THE FRENCH TEACHER | 91 |
| XXII. | ROCINANTE | 95 |
| XXIII. | FREEDOM | 99 |
| XXIV. | FATEFUL DECISIONS | 103 |
| XXV. | UNUSUAL FRIENDSHIP | 107 |
| XXVI. | DILEMMA | 111 |
| XXVII. | BETRAYAL | 117 |
| XXVIII. | THE ACCOUNTANT | 121 |
| XXIX. | THE BACHELOR PAD | 125 |
| XXX. | THE FASHION MODEL | 127 |
| XXXI. | SERIAL MONOGAMY EVALUATED | 133 |

# CHAPTER I

# THE PURPOSE OF LIFE

Prostituting himself in his stupid high paying Corporate America job, thirty one year old Kent Adams looks at his life. Two wonderful children and a marriage that leaves a lot to be desired. Eight years of mistresses to keep his ego going and now in love with the boss's secretary. Kent is bewildered with the entire mess as he walks into his 8' X 10' office with floor to ceiling beige steel walls. There is not even a window. It is eight O'clock in the morning and a sunny day outside. He shuts the door for privacy in his cold steel cell and stares at the wall. He sits at his desk having his coffee staring at the closed door. He looks around at the interior of his Spartan office and mutters aloud, "Why?" "Why am I here?" "This place is so unnatural."

"No sunlight. It is such a nice day outside and I don't even have a window. This seems like a prison with high pay. The only difference is I can go home every night where prisoners cannot. The end of each day is dark and I missed another day of sunshine in my life, and I do all this only for success".

"What is my real purpose?"

"What is the purpose of life?"

The boss's secretary comes by and knocks on the door; she is very, very beautiful with big bright eyes, brown hair and only 19.

"Hi Kent, how about a coffee? I'll buy."

"No thanks, Carol. I already have one. I need to be alone today, I have a lot of thinking to do."

"Meet you for lunch then, Carol inquires?"

"Go with the girls today, I will not be good company."

Carol closes the door quietly and Kent now holds his head up with his elbows on the desk and hands on his chin in deep thought. He eventually takes a small pad and scribbles on it:

## "WHAT IS THE PURPOSE OF LIFE?"

Later at 4:30 in the afternoon.

Carol knocks on the door. "Come in."

She sees lots of balls of crumpled paper all over the desk but notices a smile on Kent's face.

"You had no lunch she said, I left you alone like you asked."

"Help me clean this mess Carol and I will take you out for a drink."

"You were so depressed this morning and you seem so happy now. What's going on Kent?"

"I wrote a logic statement or a poem, whatever you prefer to call it. It is only four lines, but it will change my life. I will read it to you over a cocktail to see what you think of it and give you a copy to take home if you like it."

They clean up the mess and leave together.

Sitting at a table in a cocktail lounge, Kent reads the poem to Carol.

"The poem is called, In One Word"

"Like keep it simple, right?

"Right, Carol". "It answers four questions about life in just a single word". "Listen, here goes:

"What is the purpose of Life?"

"Love!"

"What is Success"?

"Happiness!"

"What is Happiness?"

"Love!"

"What is Love?"

"Giving!"

"Kent, that is so beautiful. No wonder you are so happy now".

"I know, it took me all day and it will change my life from this day forward".

"Like how?"

"I have to get out of this job". "The only thing I like about this job is the money and you".

"You know I want to get married". "Marry me"!

"I love you Carol, but I can't. I am too old for you."

"I have never touched you and I won't, it would be taking advantage of you".

"It is just the way I have been brought up".

"No you are not Kent". "Dale wants to marry me, and he is 39. You are only 31 closer to my age".

"I have a wife and two children, Carol. Eventually maybe, but I have so much to straighten out in my life, that will take some time".

"Well, I want to get married now," Carol exclaimed.

"I can't promise you anything Carol". "I only just discovered myself today".

They kiss.

The next day Kent and Carol on their lunch hour walking down the main street of White Plains, NY. Kent sings a song in her ear.

"Can't take my eyes off of you. You are like heaven to touch."

"You know Kent, you are so easy to figure out."

"How's that?"

"You wear your heart on your sleeve!"

"As long as only you see it Carol, I don't care."

"I have to go to the Federal Building to pick up tax forms for Dale."

"OK, I'll go with you."

They pick up tax forms and are alone on the elevator when Kent hits the stop button. They kiss passionately and finally start the elevator again and leave the building and walk down the street, laughing

"I love you Kent, you are so crazy."

"Don't get married Carol, wait for me to straighten out my life."

"Dale and I have set a date we are getting married soon and will move to Florida right away. So it is now or never Kent. Leave your wife and I will call the wedding off."

"You would do that for me?"

Carol starts crying on the sidewalk and Kent puts his arm around her to console her.

"Yes. It is now or never."

Emotionally upset:

"I can't. I can't. I love you Carol and it is not the time."

# CHAPTER II

# 1970 CORPORATE AMERICA

Two years later, Carol now 21 marries her fiancé Dale and they plan a move to Florida. Although Kent went to the wedding he is devastated by his own inaction and can't bear the thought of working without Carol.

Days later at work.

"I have to get out of here Carol. Will you help me?"

"Of course I will."

"Well, here is the plan. Corporate Headquarters was looking for an expert on Information Systems when they hired me. They promised me that if I took the job here for a year that they would transfer me to any location of my choice and I chose Vermont where my wife came from as the perfect place to bring up my children."

"What can I do?" inquired Carol.

"It is your boss that made me this offer two years ago not the idiot that I currently work for. What they fear most around here is an open door letter of complaint to the Chairman of the Board.

Heads will roll if the management is found at fault, especially here in Corporate Headquarters."

"You are right about that" offers Carol.

"I have written an Open Door Letter to the Chairman complaining that management broke its promise to me. I don't want to send it because I like your boss and wish him no harm. However, the letter will have the same effect if you told your boss that you typed the letter for me, and you warn him of this letter out of loyalty for him as his secretary."

"What do you think Carol?"

"That just might work, I'll do it."

The next day at the Corporate Offices, Carol's boss Dave visits Kent's office.

"Hello Kent. I have some news for you."

"Hi Dave. How's it going?"

"I have been in touch with the personnel department in Burlington, Vermont and they have scheduled a few interviews for you.

"Well thank you Dave, when do I go?"

"Next Monday. Sorry it took me so long, but you have been getting paid far more then their salary scale has permitted in the past. It is only now that Burlington is growing that it might be possible to fit you in up there."

"I understand and appreciate your effort Dave. I'll do my best to get a job up there. I appreciate you keeping your promise."

"Starting today, you report directly to me and not to Phil any longer. We are looking into Phil's management ability and treatment of employees at this very moment."

"Thank you Dave. I'll keep you posted."

Dave leaves Kent's office and shortly thereafter Carol arrives.

"Well?"

"Thank you, Carol. It worked. No hassle. Dave has already set up interviews for me in Burlington, Vermont."

"I'll bet you will be in Burlington, Vermont before I move to Florida," says Carol.

"I can't work here without you. I will eventually straighten out my life. I have no idea how long it will take. I will visit you and Dale in Florida and the both of you can visit us in Vermont. In fact this weekend why don't you and Dale come for dinner at our home across the river in New Jersey and we can celebrate both of our upcoming moves.

# CHAPTER III

# VERMONT

## BURLINGTON, VERMONT

The new Laboratory offices are under construction and the company has rented temporary quarters in the old brick buildings of Fort Ethan Allen. Kent is talking to his new boss.

"Well Kent, how do you like Burlington so far."

"I Love it Al. The company took good care of me. They paid for my move, allowed me to house hunt, gave me a raise to come here and I am very happy to work for you."

"I heard you bought a house already."

"Yes Al, a four bedroom ranch in Colchester. There is not a single traffic light between my home and work. However, I do have to stop for cows crossing the street sometimes."

"Ha. You are quite familiar with Corporate Headquarters and I would like you to act as liaison for Management Information Systems, by traveling to these Westchester sites from time to time."

"Sure, I would like that, I still have friends there."

Kent is on a business trip to Westchester, Carol takes the day off and they meet for lunch in a Delicatessen in Greenwich, CT.

"It is so good to see you again Carol."

"Are you happy Kent?"

"I am working on it. I sure blew it with you."

"We never had an affair Kent and thank goodness, all we did was kiss. I still want to kiss you, and feel so good about you. You have always treated me as your ideal woman as if I were on a pedestal and unattainable by you. Many women never see that in their entire life. I am so thankful for you and the way you handled my affection for you. You are such a gentlemen and I will always love you."

"I have to learn to live without you Carol. I hope you and Dale are happy."

"Yes we are. We move to Florida next month. I hope you find a woman to love so you can put your poem into practice and lead the life that you have defined for yourself."

Kent sings softly:"Can't take my eyes off of you".

Carol with her eyes watering:"Eventually you will achieve your goal of living a life of love without any guilt."

"I hope so, Carol. Vermont is a good first step, and a wonderful environment to bring up my children. It is very important for me to make sure that if I ever get the courage to leave my wife that they have a good life with their father always available to them nearby."

"You will find that right woman, when you least expect it, and when that happens, you will once again have to deal with your own morality. It is your high moral standards that cause you so much guilt."

# CHAPTER V

# FASCINATION

Working now at old Fort Ethan Allen in Vermont. Kent walks past a narrow wooden staircase and sees a beautiful young redhead woman dressed in a red and white blouse and blue mini-skirt outfit. She is coming down the old wooden staircase where Kent is waiting at the bottom. He tries not to look up her dress but he does anyway out of curiosity.

"Hi, where do you work?"

"Upstairs, I am a secretary in the personnel department. Are you new here?"

"Yes, I transferred from Corporate Headquarters. My name is Kent, what's yours?"

"Kim. What do you do?"

"I am a system designer trying to design an Information System for Burlington."

"Have to go now, nice to meet you," Kim responds.

Kent watches her walk down the hallway to the copy machine, fascinated by how skinny she is, while at the same time thinking of her big blue eyes and Irish beauty, her smile and her long red hair past her shoulders captivate him. The next day Kent is at his desk in front of the old fashioned roll up window when he sees a car pull up to the old fort building. He sees Kim's very handsome husband give her a kiss as she gets out of the car and comes into the building.

"Hi Kent."

"Hi Kim, you shouldn't kiss in public."

"Ha! My VW is in the shop, so my husband had to drive me."

"Can, I take you to lunch?"

"Sure, I will be down at noon."

Kim climbs the stairs.

A little after noon having lunch in a small restaurant.

"Where do you live Kim?

"Duxbury, in the woods."

"Do you like the country?"

"I love it, it is so peaceful."

"What does your husband do?"

"He builds houses. He built our house in the woods."

"How's your job?"

"It is Okay. I was trained as a legal secretary in secretarial school so it is easy for me. A lot of secretaries here have only on the job training."

The next day, Kim is at the copy machine and Kent walks up to her and asks:

"How about lunch again today?"

"I have my own car today. Why don't I meet you at the same restaurant. We should not be seen together anyway."

"Okay. Good idea" answers Kent.

At the restaurant, sitting in a corner table for lunch.

"Kent, tell me about you. I see your ring so I know you are married."

"Yes. I have been married 11 years now. I have two beautiful children. The eldest Monica at eight years old and Stephen who is five. We live in Mallets Bay in Colchester about two blocks from the Boat club."

"Do you love your wife?"

"I have tried to, but I don't."

"I don't love my husband either."

"Why?"

"He is not faithful to me. He calls me too skinny. He goes out with 18 year olds and lies to me all the time."

"How old are you?"

"Twenty six."

"I just finished a platonic relationship with a beautiful 21 year old, I met her at 19 and thought she was too young for me so we never had sex and I must be a jerk because she married someone eight years older than me."

"You were hurt by that?"

"Yes, very much, I thought I would be taking advantage of her so I only kissed her. I wouldn't be in Vermont now if it wasn't for her, she was the perfect friend that I needed at that time."

"Why don't you love your wife, Kent?"

"We have no conununication."

"Why is that?"

"She continually uses her favorite expression that she thinks ends all communication."

"What is that?

"Too bad you feel that way!"

"As if somehow you are not thinking clearly?"

"No it is more like, this conversation is over, screw you!"

"Wow, I understand. How do you reply?"

"I just smile and think to myself about my two beautiful children as the only reason I keep this dysfunctional marriage going, when in fact it is too bad for Darla because without open communication, it is only a matter of time before my responsibility to my children will be over."

They leave the restaurant and walk to the VW parked outside. Kent opens the door for Kim and she gets in. She rolls down the window to say good bye. Kent leans over to kiss her and they kiss. She smiles and leaves the parking lot with the putt, putt noise of a Volkswagen accelerating.

The next day. Kent sees Kim in the hallway with a package from the mailroom and inquires:"Lunch today?"

"No. Too dangerous for you Kent. How about after work? I can meet you for an hour."

"Okay. Park your car at the train station and I will pick you up."

"All right."

Kent's car pulls up next to the red Volkswagen at the Train Station. Kim gets out and gets in Kent's car. They hold hands. Kim says, "Let's go somewhere where we can be alone."

"Okay Kim, I know a deserted fishing access on the Winooski River."

They pull into the fishing access and park the car. Kim grabs Kent and they steam up the windows kissing.

"You are beautiful Kim."

"I feel so good when I am with you Kent."

"I need you so much Kim, I am so lost, I want you."

"No. Not now, not here. Tomorrow."

"Where?"

"Get a motel room. I will give myself to you there, you can have anything you want but not here in the car."

"Okay. Tomorrow," says Kent. "How late can you stay out?"

"Maybe until 9:00 O'clock. I will say a girlfriend invited me to use her pool after work."

"Oh, how I look forward to being alone with you. The Company gives us no privacy at all. We are both in terror waiting to be discovered at lunch."

"For me Kent it is not so bad, but for your career it would be devastating to get caught. You will be fired."

"Do you know that when I first joined this company it was forbidden to have even a beer at lunch.We all wore blue suits, white shirts and standard ties. Corporate America types all looked alike."

"Vermont is a little bit more relaxed Kent, but when it comes to sex with an employee they would fire us both."

"I need you so much Kim; the risk will be worth it."

"Where will we go Kent?"

"Not in Burlington, too easy to be seen. We will head out towards Barre and find a motel."

"Okay for tomorrow," she says.

"Are you sure Kim?"

"I am sure."

They kiss passionately.

# CHAPTER VI

# INTERLUDE

A fleabag motel, probably built in the 1930s, in Barre Vermont. Kent shuts the door behind them. Kim walks to the window and closes the curtains because it is still daylight.

"Alone at last," says Kent. They hug and kiss.

"Open the champagne Kent. I can use some to relax my nerves."

"Sure. I am as nervous as you are, so relax."

She takes off her blouse and bra as Kent watches her refer to her breasts.

"They are not very big, but they work."

"Ha. Ha. What a sense of humor."

Kent pops the Champagne cork into a towel and pours the bubbles into fluted glasses. She gets completely naked and sits on the bed. Kent hands her a glass of champagne and says: "You are very beautiful. I can see now that you really are a redhead. HA! From now on I will call you BIG RED. A toast to you and I, BIG RED!"

"To us."

"To us."

Kent gets undressed and puts her glass down and they kiss and roll over and make love so beautifully and passionately that is seems they are made for each other.

Kent, driving the car alone and mumbling to himself on the ride home.

"What am I doing? She is so skinny, almost anorexic. Maybe it is just a one night stand and I should forget about it. A real nice gal at any rate. It is like making love to a twig. What, am I crazy?"

At work the next day.

"Kent, wipe that smile off your face."

"Ha. You make me happy Kim."

"I know I do. You make me happy too. I can only get away like that once a week. In the meantime I can spend about an hour with you every day after work. Is that all right?"

"Of course."

"We will eventually get caught at the fishing access Kent. Do you have any other ideas?"

"It is summertime, so we are lucky. I know a very romantic spot close to here where we can park our cars and walk in a field of daisies. Follow me after work and I will show you."

"Stop smiling, you are like a little boy."

About 5:00 P.M. A field of daisies on a hill with a lone dead tree at the top. The two cars are parked on the dirt road and Kim and Kent are holding hands walking through the field to the top of the hill.

"What a beautiful spot."

"I thought you would like it Kim."

"I can get away again tomorrow night."

"Great. I found a better motel. It is also closer than Barre."

"Where Kent?"

"It is in Waterbury, Between Stowe and Sugarbush but it is only 15 minutes by interstate highway? It is close to your home in Duxbury, we will have more time together. A few doors away there is a church where you can leave your car and we can meet so I can take to the motel."

"So far, so good, no one has seen us."

They sit down on top of the hill surrounded by flowers and kiss and talk.

At Waterbury Motel. They have finished making love and are drinking champagne and eating cheese.

"I love you Kent."

"Kim our secret life will take its toll. We can not even go to a restaurant or we will be seen together and the gossip will start. Living in fear of getting caught will take its toll and will wear us down. I certainly can afford to take you out and show you off."

"I'm happy here Kent. Champagne and cheese is fine with me. I am easy to please. I don't have to go out to dinner. A toast to you Kent. I heard you got promoted, it was on the bulletin board."

"Thank you. They made me manager which is a big promotion for me. I am now Manager of a brand new systems department in the Laboratory."

"Wow. Impressive." Kim smiles.

"I have requisitions for five new people and I want you to be my secretary."

"My boss will never let me go."

"I'll take care of it, if you want me to."

"Of course I do. I love you."

Kent drops her off at her VW in the church parking lot. He opens the car door for her and she gets in the VW. He kisses her and she drives off. He gets back in his own car and starts for home, muttering to himself as he drives.

19

•

"I really love her. I am smitten. She has invaded my soul, we are so compatible. I remember the last time I drove home and I wasn't sure. Now I am absolutely sure."

"I love her."

"I truly love her!

Lunch time, the next day. Kent is driving Kim to the modern new building which is now ready for occupancy.

"What are you smiling about?"

"I love you Kim."

"You feel like you have conquered me don't you?

"Well you let me. We conquered each other and I smile because of how good I feel about you."

"Well stop smiling, people will notice. You're whole face lights up when you see me."

"Kim, your Boss will probably tell you this afternoon that you will be transferred to my department."

"How did you do that?"

"I just let the Personnel Department handle it, by letting them know it is a growth opportunity for you. They spoke to your boss as if he would be holding you back from a career opportunity if he did not consent."

"Where are we going?"

"To our new offices in the new building so I can show you where you will be working as my secretary."

"When do we move?"

"The movers will have us moved in by Monday morning."

"I'm so excited, new job, new building, and working with you. Wow!"

# CHAPTER VI

# THE SECRETARY

The next week, they are settled in a suite of offices on the second floor in the Southeast corner of the new building with large windows and a great view of the Green Mountain Range. There is a secretarial bay for two secretaries. Kim's desk is right outside the door of Kent's office. The other desk is for Kent's manager's secretary.

"Good morning Kent. This sure beats working in that old Fort Ethan Allen."

"You like it, huh?"

"In my wildest imagination I still don't believe it."

"It is the start of a new life for both of us. We have a department meeting in the conference room in five minutes, will you be ready?"

"Yes, I'm ready".

The conference room.

The employees are sitting at a long table and Kent is introducing the employees to each other and asking each of them to tell the group about themselves. Kim is sitting opposite Kent and is smiling in

admiration of Kent as the meeting progresses. Kent can actually
feel her smile as her eyes caress him in front of everyone. No one
but Kent notices.

That evening at the motel in Waterbury.
Kent is in bed after making love to Kim. She is in the bathroom with
the door open slightly. He looks around the room and sees that the
only light in the room comes from the old time radio and from the
bathroom door open just a crack. The light from the radio shines
on the wine bottle and glasses half full of the red wine and the red
wax covered Edam cheese showing the bright yellow chunks cut on
a plate on the end table. Kim turns the light out in he bathroom and
comes out naked.

"Do you love me?" she asks.

"What do you think? You want to make love again?"

"Yes."

"I love you Kim. Till death do us part."

"Don't get morbid. Will you marry me?"

"I will have to get divorced first."

"Well get divorced. You don't love your wife do you?"

"No. As the mother of my children she is fine. As a wife, a
disaster. We have no sex whatsoever. I only love you."

"When did you stop loving your wife?"

"About six months after we were married, we were returning to
New Jersey from a sports car race in West Virginia when she
told me that she had gone out on me when we were engaged. It
made me feel as if I got married under false pretenses. I tried to
explain my disappointment and we had a big argument and she
went home to see her mother for about ten days."

"That's crazy. What did you do?"

"I was working in New Jersey for ITT at the time and I had an
affair with my secretary the entire time she was gone."

"How long did that last?"

"On and off for more than ten years and right up until I met you."

"What do you mean on and off?"

"Well I would so feel guilty and sometimes I would not see her for three years at a time while I tried to make my marriage work. About five years ago, she got married, but that didn't matter, all I had to do was call her and she would be there for me. Hey, I am not perfect. I do not like myself for it. Someday I would like to marry you and straighten out my life."

"We are going to hurt so many people Kent."

"I know, I have been brought up Catholic, I believe in the Ten Commandments and I have a lot of trouble accepting myself knowing that right now I am in violation of two commandments."

"I know of one, Thou Shalt Not Commit Adultery."

"Yes Kim, the other is Thou Shalt Not Covet Thy Neighbor's Wife."

"Oh, Kent, you are right I forgot that one.

"I can't imagine my parents accepting a divorce."

"Mine too."

"I love my children very much and just the thought of breaking up my family is devastating. It is not fair to my children. They need a father"

"You can still be a good father if you make yourself accessible to your children. I accept your children, we can make it together. Marry me!"

"I love you Kim. I will marry you, right now before God."

"What does that mean?"

"I will show you. Kneel with me next to the bed."

They get out of bed naked and kneel with their elbows on the bed as if saying their prayers.

"I love you Kent."

"Dear God. I love Kim and pledge to love her until death do us part as God is my witness." "Please consider us married from this day forward. We both appear before you naked as you created us and want to pledge or lives to each other with your blessing until we both get a divorce from our present spouse. I will eventually resolve a divorce from Darla whom I can not love. Kim, do you take me as your husband from this day forward?"

"Yes. I do."

"God is our witness."

They get up and sip the Bordeaux wine and kiss and smile at each other.

"I am so happy Kent. I guess we don't need a piece of paper saying we are married."

Each morning Kim has coffee waiting for Kent when he arrives for work. When he sits at his desk she stands next to him so close that their legs touch. He invariably puts his hand up her mini skirt to pet her. She smiles and laughs every time.

"You have to stop buying me coffee."

"I insist. I learned it in Secretarial School."

"Can I leave money in the drawer for you to buy it?

"No! Hey, did you hear!"

"What?"

"Pete, your boss's boss, left his wife. Wants a divorce."

"A Senior Engineer. The first divorce of a high level manager in Burlington. What a scandal."

"Everybody's talking. He has been dating on the sly for a year and he served papers on his wife yesterday and moved out."

"It will be interesting to see the company reaction. He is the first one in management to seek a divorce. I like him a lot. He has helped my career. I hope it does not ruin his career."

"I am afraid it will, Kent."

"When I worked for a Santa Monica, California Corporation, I met a lot of divorced people. I guess because as a California

Company divorce is more accepted there. But, this is Corporate America, where scandal ruins your career and it is also Vermont where divorce is almost unheard of in 1970. It is only now that I can have a beer with my lunch in a restaurant and I can finally wear colored shirts without Big Brother the Company criticizing me."

"You will be next, right Kent?"

"Well, let's allow Pete to be the test case."

"You won't even have lunch with me in the cafeteria, and you are thinking divorce? Ha!"

"You really want to start rumors, don't you? I have lunch with fellow employees and men only. You eat with the women so nobody suspects us. Call it part of our suffering."

"The weather is approaching winter Kent. The daises on the hilltop are dead. What will we do after work every day?"

"I know, it is getting cold. We will just have to neck in the car."

"I can't believe we haven't been caught. I don't care, I'll go anywhere with you, I love you Kent."

The Motel in Waterbury: It is Kent's birthday.

Kent is in bed and notices that the only light is again coming from the radio, and from a tiny crack from the bathroom door that allows a narrow ray of light to escape. Kim shuts off the bathroom light and enters the room naked and singing holding a cup cake with a candle lit on top."Happy Birthday to you."

"You gotta be kidding, how did you know?"

"I'm your secretary. I know everything about you. Make a wish!"

"Okay. I wish we could find a way to be married now."

"You are not supposed to tell me your wish. I knew it anyway. Ha!"

"I love you Kim."

"I know it. You make me feel loved. My whole body quivers

when I am with you. You gave me 10 organisms tonight, our new record. At 9 I thought I could do no more but you said go for it. After 10, I pleaded with you to stop before I had a heart attack. We must be crazy."

"Kim, you are like a Stradivarius Violin, and we make love in concert together. I get my satisfaction from pleasing you. You are a perfect ten!"

"I get the pun on ten, my heart was beating so fast I thought I would die. Good God, I love you Kent." They kiss.

"Here Kent open this little gift, it's not much at all but it is something to remember me by." Kent gives Kim a hug and slowly unwraps the gift.

"Hey, a coffee cup that says LEO, thank you."

"You are a Leo, Kent so when I get you your morning coffee, it will be in a Leo cup."

"Thanks Kim, I love you so much."

"Me too!"

# CHAPTER VII

# SUGARBUSH

It is winter now on the Sugarbush Vermont ski trails where Kim starts the introductions.

"Kent and Darla, this is my husband Frank."

"Nice to meet you Frank, these are my children Monica and Stephen. I understand you are on the Ski patrol."

"Yes, I guess Kim told you. How are your kids doing?"

"They have previously been skiing at Madonna, Bolton Valley, Jay Peak and Stowe. They took a week ski lessons at Stowe last year and will take a week here in Sugarbush this year."

"We live close by, so we will be here every day. If I can help at all, please let me know."

Frank takes off skiing down the trail.

"Kim, he seems like such a nice guy."

"Be careful Kent, he is a salesman. Let me go skiing with your kids while you and Darla attempt Castle Rock. I'll keep and eye on them, until they start their ski lessons, then I will meet you on the mountain."

"Thank you Kim," says Darla. "Very nice of you."

Later in the day on the top of Castle Rock Frank skis up to Kent.

"How are you doing Kent."

"Not so good, Frank. I am afraid of the glade."

"You ski all right. What are you afraid of?"

"I will hit a tree, for sure."

"Follow me; I will give you some tips."

Frank heads down and stops, waiting now for Kent. Kent starts down and stops near Frank.

"I told you, I am no good at this."

"Let's go only 20 feet keeping your knees together and your skis parallel. Use the steel edges of your skis to stop on a dime."

Kent tries it and it works.

"Wow, it works."

"Now let's move into complete parallel skiing, you have the idea, just use the steel edges to grab the surface to the point of stopping if you need to and jump turn keeping your skis parallel."

"A free lesson from a pro, thanks Frank."

By the end of the day Frank and Kent are seen skiing effortlessly through the glade. By the end of the week at Sugarbush after ski lessons for the kids they are happily skiing the beginners' slopes. Frank, Kim, Darla and Kent are skiing Castle Rock and occasionally meeting each other.

"Darla, did you enjoy your week?" asked Kim.

"I sure did. Everyone in the family has improved their skiing this year. Especially Kent. Frank has been a good help to him."

"I am sure glad you came to Sugarbush instead of Stowe. As Kent's secretary I speak to you on the telephone all the time, and meeting you makes it so much more personal.

"Yes, Darla says. Now I know who I am talking to. Sugrbush is beautiful. We had a great week. The kids learned a lot, I feel comfortable skiing and Kent is afraid of no mountain with the instruction Frank gave him. I think he did every slope on Castle Rock and can't wait to do the Nose Dive at Stowe.

Back at work Kim and Kent are looking out the window at the parking lot with plows pushing the snow around.

"Look at all that snow Kent. We can't go to Waterbury today, it will be too dangerous on the interstate."

"Let's take a chance and go to the Holiday Inn right here in Burlington. I will check in and come out to the parking lot and get you."

"That's pretty dangerous Kent. Some of the employees go to the bar there for happy hour."

"You can wait in the car in the parking lot while I check in. I will come down and give you the key and we can go in separately and meet in the room."

"Sounds dangerous Kent, but okay."

"There is a foot of snow on my car and I don't even have a brush."

"I do Kim says, I will clean your car off."

The Corporate Parking Lot.

Kim wearing a designer wool hat with a pom pom on it with a matching scarf over her coat, comes over with a brush to clean Kent's car. Her cheeks are red from the cold and she looks absolutely beautiful.

"God, you are beautiful. I can't wait to get you to the hotel."

"Ha. I think you thrive on danger."

She sweeps the snow off Kent's car and they leave in separate cars.

The Holiday Inn, Burlington.

Kent is already in the room and the door opens and Kim comes in. Kent takes off her heavy coat and pulls the pom pom to take her hat off. Her long red hair falls to her shoulders. They kiss and fall to the bed. After and hour of love making they are just talking to each other under the covers. Kim appears very serious.

"I don't want to go home tonight Kent."

"I don't want to go home tonight either."

"My husband is getting suspicious, he doesn't believe I have an art class during the winter and have been using a friend's swimming pool in the summer. He now calls me a whore. It hurts me because it is not true. I have never been with anyone but you and my husband and I need to be with you always because I love you."

"Be patient Kim, we will find a way."

"Call your wife now and say you are not coming home ever again, and I will call Frank and say the same thing. It is that easy. Do it!"

"Kim, you would do that now, tonight?"

"Yes. I want to feel good about myself."

"I can't call now, but I can start letting my wife know that I intend to leave her, so she can make preparations."

"Promise me Kent, you will do that?"

"I promise. Hey, let's order dinner from Room Service. Finally, we are in a hotel that is not a flea bag."

"Ha. Okay. I love you."

At work, weeks later.

"Kim, because the Laboratory must reduce headcount my entire department is being transferred to Manufacturing Information Systems."

"Is that good?"

"No. It is bad. I will have a manager who I have no respect for, and his manager is even worse. It will be a hostile environment for us. Instead of having a small talented department of 6 people, I inherit the existing Administrative Systems Department of 21 additional people. What a nightmare."

"I will help you, we will get through this."

# CHAPTER VIII

# INSUBORDINATION

The transfer takes place and Kent's department is transferred from the Lab to Manufacturing. Kent's new boss Doug calls Kent in to his office.

"Welcome, Kent to Manufacturing Information Systems. Over here we have a head count crunch and each department has to isolate at least one person to be fired. First, you put the person on notice. Second, you put enough pressure on them that they either quit or are fired. One of the people you inherited, Glen Jones, has already been put on notice, so your job is to get him out of your department and reduce your head count. Still another one that you brought with you in the transfer probably should be put on notice, because I never liked that Fred La Motte. He is a trouble maker. Get rid of him."

"Well, I will look into it Doug."

Back in Kent's New Office, Kim asks, "How did it go?"

"This place is like Nazi Germany. There is a purge going on here. I am supposed to fire people who don't measure up to

Doug's standards, rather than the company's standard. Doug is a tyrant dictator."

"It is not like the lab is it?"

"No, totally different management caused by too much nepotism over the years. The management here has been together so long that they watch out for each other. I am clearly an outsider."

Days later in Kent's Office

"What's the matter Kim you look upset?" Kim's hands are shaking.

"Doug, your boss's boss followed me halfway home last night. He was right on my tail and I couldn't shake him. I could see his face clearly in the rear view mirror.

"Do you think he suspects us and he wants to see if we meet someplace?"

"I don't know, but I was scared. The pervert gives me the creeps. It could be he wants attention from me as he made no effort to hide. He wants me to ask him why he follows me."

"If that's the case, say nothing to him about it. If it happens again, let me know. That's called stalking and I will do something about it. You are a beautiful woman and I am not surprised by his behavior."

"Thanks Kent, I feel better now."

# CHAPTER IX

# **COMMITMENT**

The hilltop full of daisies. Kim and Kent are sitting on top of the hill talking and kissing.

"Oh Kent, Spring is here again. I just love this time of year."

"Yeah. The mating season. I want you bad."

"You are always joking, have you told your wife yet that you are leaving."

"Yes. She plays games. Her game is she doesn't believe me. I asked her months ago to make whatever preparations she needs because sometime within this year I will be gone. Do you think a year is enough?

"Of course, she manipulates you."

"I know it."

"I have decided to leave Frank. I already told my mother and she understands. I want to rent a summer cottage in Malletts bay to be near you."

"I will leave too then, I want to be with you."

"No. Frank does not know about you. I want to leave to be a

free woman and not for another man. It just creates unnecessary jealously. It will be easier on everybody if I leave alone. You can be with me but don't leave until I am already single and settled."

"When, Kim? When will you do this?"

"The day after your birthday. It's your present. We will be together a little over a year. I will take the day off from work to move."

"The best year of my life, Kim."

Kent is summoned to Doug's Office at work.

"You wanted to see me Doug?"

"I will be on vacation for the next two weeks. How are you doing with reducing head count?"

"I have been working on it. Glen is in New York today with an interview."

"That's not the way to do it Kent. I want him fired, not transferred. You are just giving someone else the problem."

"I have observed his work closely the past few months and he does not deserve to be fired. His acne is not easy to look at but it does not affect his work. The problem is medical only. He is a contributing part of the team."

"Get rid of him Kent, also now that my secretary has quit I will be transferring your secretary to my office to replace her when I return from vacation. You can share Bill's secretary."

"Kim is scheduled for promotion to systems analyst. You will be hurting her career."

"Kent, you protect her too much. She is a trained executive secretary and belongs in my department."

It is Kent's Birthday. He is sitting on the side stoop of his home contemplating the three four foot stalks for the future sunflowers he planted in the two foot square plot of dirt between the garage and the side stoop of his home in Colchester. He has a can of beer in his hand and is in deep thought as his wife, son and daughter approach from the neighbor's house next door. Monica is holding a birthday cake which she obviously baked next door, with 32 candles lit and they are all singing."Happy Birthday to you."

Kent, knowing that he will soon leave his children, starts crying uncontrollably in front of his children.

"Did you bake that cake Monica?"

"Yeah, Dad. Happy Birthday."

Kent puts his arms around the two children and can not control his tears.

"What is the matter Kent?" Says Darla.

"You know what I have to do, it is so difficult for me. I love my children so much."

"You need a doctor. I'll make an appointment for tomorrow."

It is Friday morning. Kent is alone at work because Kim has the day off. The telephone rings and Darla is on the line.

"Kent, I have made a Doctor' appointment for you at two O'clock this afternoon. It is the only time he can see you, so be there on time."

"Okay Darla, Where?"

"Our family doctor in Winooski."

"All right, I'll be there."

He hangs up and the phone rings again.

"Hello. Kent here."

"Hi, it's me. I have already left Frank, I am calling from my mother's house.

"What did he say?"

"I don't know. I left him a note."

"Wow, Kim. What's next?"

"I will go and find a place in Mallets Bay, near you and I will call you and let you know where I am so we can be together tonight."

"Well Kim, don't call here this afternoon, Darla made a Doctor's appointment for me and I won't be at work.

"Okay. I'll call you when I am ready."

Kent makes his appointment at the Doctors Office.

"Hello Kent, why do you think you are here?"

"Hi Doc, to please my wife I guess."

"I'm just a general practitioner and I would like to refer you to Dr. Hayes if it is all right with you."

"What for?"

"He is a psychiatrist, and I believe you will find him very helpful. He is an older gentleman with great credentials, actually I think, one of the best in Burlington."

"A shrink? I'm not crazy."

"Probably not, but give him a try, you will learn about yourself. I set an appointment for you on Monday at three in the afternoon."

Kent's leaves the doctors office and goes home.

"What did the doctor tell you?" Darla asks.

"He referred me to a shrink. But it is too late, I am leaving tonight."

"Where are you going to go?"

"I don't know, but I am leaving."

The phone rings and Darla answers.

"Who was that, Darla?"

"I don't know, it was a hang up. The third one today. So you are leaving tonight, but you don't know where you are going. Sounds like a shrink is what you need.

When is your appointment?"

"Monday at Three".

"Good. Make sure you go."

Monday morning after a bad weekend waiting for Kim's call

to learn where she is. Kent enters his office to find Kim crying hysterically:

"Where were you?"

"Calm down Kim. I waited for your call all night. I was worried."

He shuts the door behind her as she cries profusely. He tries to put his arm around her but she pushes him away.

"I called the office and they said you were gone for the afternoon."

"I told you I would not be in all afternoon because I had a doctor appointment."

"I called your house and your wife answered."

"Why didn't you just ask for me?"

"I was afraid."

"I already told my wife I was leaving Friday night, but I didn't know where to go. You never told me."

Now they are both in tears.

"I couldn't reach you, I was going crazy so I called the hospital and committed myself to the whacko ward. The next day my mother came and got me out."

"Are you back with Frank?"

"Yes."

Kim is again in hysterics, her hands are shaking.

"What can I do to help you?"

"Nothing!"

"Kim, what a story. I love you Kim and I did tell my wife I was leaving that evening. I had no idea where to go, so I looked like a jerk, she thought I was crazy. Please take the day off, go home and rest. You are too upset to be here today. Thanks for coming in to let me know what happened. Doug is on vacation and he wants you to be his secretary in two weeks when he returns."

"That creep! I can't work for him."

"I will do what I can to save you from that."

"I just don't care any more."

Kent dries her eyes. "Come on, I'll walk you to your car."

"No, I'll go myself."

She opens the door and leaves. Kent picks up the telephone.

"Dorothy, please. Hello, Dorothy. This is Kent. For a year now I have been privileged to have Kim for my secretary which I thank you sincerely for."

"I know Kent, she is very talented."

"She has nothing but the highest ratings. In fact she is so good she should be working for someone much higher up in the executive ladder than me."

"It is always nice to get feedback on the people I place. Thanks Kent.

"I am in a position now where I have to cut my Headcount and Kim enjoyed so much the lab environment much more than here in manufacturing. As much as I would hate to lose Kim I would like to help her if I can. Would you please investigate any executive secretarial openings in the Lab for me? I am sure she would appreciate anything you and I could do for her."

"Actually Kent your timing is perfect. I know of a Lab opening right now working for Third Level Manager which could get her a promotion as well. Do you want me to set up an interview for Kim?"

"Yes. Thank you. She is out today and probably tomorrow, but Wednesday will be fine. She is so good that she deserves the job and a promotion. I am glad I called you Dorothy."

"Stay in touch Kent."


Kent enters the psychiatrist's office and notices the elderly Doctor behind his desk. Kent looks around the room and at all the nice furniture with sofas and chairs.

"Welcome Kent. Have a seat."

Kent selects a straight back wooden chair close to the doctor's desk.

"Hello, Doctor."

"How can I be of help?"

"My wife sent me here. She thinks I'm crazy because I want to leave her."

"Well Kent, what do you think about that?"

"I'm not crazy; I am in love with another woman."

"Tell me about her, what's her name?"

"Kim."

Kent relates the entire story up until today.

"It probably is a good day for you to be here. You have had a lot of problems today."

"Yeah, I guess the timing is sort of perfect to be here."

Kent breaks down and cries.

"We have been going for more then two hours Kent. My sessions are usually one hour once a week. Instead of waiting for next Monday why don't you come in again this Friday at 3:00 P.M. Can you possibly get a week off from work?"

"It is not a good time, my boss is out. Why do you ask?"

"I would prefer then that you make no decisions at work of any consequence. Can you shut your office door and not see anyone for awhile."

"Yes."

"Well do that for a couple of weeks. I'll see you on Friday."


Two weeks later, Kent is summoned to Doug's Office.

"Hi Doug. How was your vacation?"

Doug is visibly shaken and violently angry.

"What is going on Kent? In my absence, you transferred Kim back to the Lab. That's insubordination."

"No it isn't Doug. She was offered a promotion, you didn't mention a promotion for her."

"I might have." Doug's hands are trembling.

"Well you should have told me. When one of my people is offered

a promotion I won't hold them back. That's the corporate policy."
Kent smiles.

"What about the two people on your target list for dismissal?"

"They're gone Doug! One transferred to Boca Raton, Florida the other is back in the Lab where he came from."

Doug's face is now flush red with rage. "Effective Monday Kent, you are being replaced. You will be excess baggage in limbo waiting for the personnel department to find you a new job. I must say I have never met a more determined adversary. You know your way around this company pretty well."

"Our problem Doug, is your use of the word adversary. You never saw me as a member of your team by your own definition. Adversary, just imagine, what hypocrisy."

# CHAPTER X

# MOTHERHOOD

Weeks go by; Kim is settled in her new job. Kent is limbo in an office with no job assignment, he sees her occasionally walking through the second floor glass hallways that connects the buildings. He calls her sometimes hoping she will come to her senses. Kent is very depressed and still seeing the Psychiatrist. Kim is also now seeing a Psychiatrist. The phone rings and Kent picks it up.

"Hello."

"It's me."

"What a mess our lives are."

"Can I see you tonight?"

"Sure, where?"

"The motel in Waterbury."

"OK Kim. I'll meet you at the church."

He hangs up. The telephone rings again.

"Hello, Kent here."

"Hi, this is Dorothy. You sure did the right thing by Kim."

"I couldn't have done it without your help."

"Now, the Personnel Department is going to help you."

"Another management job?"

"No. Better. How would you like to be on the Plant Manager's Staff?"

"Yeah, that would be great. I'm tired of doing nothing."

"You have an interview with his Senior Staff Assistant tomorrow at 10:00 A.M."

"Thanks Dorothy. Wish me luck."

"You won't need it. You will get the job."

That night at the motel in Waterbury. After an hour of love making they talk.

"You sure did stick your neck out for me Kent."

"Do you like your new boss?"

"Yes he is a nice man and thankful to you for sending me there. Thank God I don't have to work for that creep Doug."

"I knew I had to move fast while Doug was on vacation."

If I didn't you would be working for him today. I'm so sorry to lose you."

"He must have been out of his mind when he found that you transferred three people while he was gone."

"He was envious of my courage. He called me his adversary, what an ignorant man. He couldn't manage me. How's life at home?"

"Not good, we argue all the time. I should have stayed in Mallets Bay when I left and was already moved in."

"We will make it Kim, just keep your eye on the goal."

Kim appears worried.

"I have to tell you something. I can't keep it inside any longer."

"Okay what?"

"I am going to Europe for six weeks."

She starts crying,

"That's why I wanted to be with you tonight. I wanted to tell you myself rather than have you looking all over for me."

"That is like saying we have no chance whatsoever."

"Frank's father is paying for the trip. He thinks it will repair our broken marriage. I must go."

Kent puts his arm around her.

"What do you think?"

"Why do you think I am here with you now? I love you."

"When do you leave?"

"Tomorrow!"

They Kiss.

Two weeks later.

Kent is carrying his tray in the cafeteria and sees Kim having lunch with her girlfriends. He walks over to talk to Kim while still standing.

"You are back already? What about the six weeks?"

"Yeah, it didn't work out."

"How's Europe, did you like it?"

"Too many old buildings for me."

"Ha. Where did you park Kim?"

"Same place."

"Follow me after work."

"Okay."

Kent leaves with his tray to join his friends for lunch.

Later in the day after work.

The two cars enter a road that has signs saying 'ROAD CLOSED, Bridge under repair.' They pull up to the bridge and get out.

"How did you find this place?"

"I went to St. Michael's College across the street when I was young. I am always looking for a nearby spot for us. When I saw that the road was closed because of the bridge repair I knew it would be a perfect scenic place for us to meet."

They walk out on the bridge high over the canyon overlooking the Winooski River.

"Oh Kent, what a beautiful place."

"So, tell me what happened on your trip."

"I don't love him. I love you. That's all there is to it. Europe wasn't helping at all so I said let's go home. I will leave him again and he knows it. Do you still want me?"

"Of course Kim, I love you."

"You promise to come to me this time."

"Yes, I promise. But tell me where you are."

"I will. Nothing will stop us now. Let me leave Frank first and be a single person and you can join me when I am single. Agreed?"

"Agreed. I will leave my wife as soon as you want me to."

"Promise Kent?"

"Promise."

They kiss.


The next week.

Kent has been calling Kim at work every day, only to find that she has been out sick all week. The following Monday when walking across the second floor glass tube connecting the buildings he sees Kim coming the other way. She is not smiling and appears troubled.

"Are you OK? Have you been sick?" Kent asks.

"I'm pregnant!"

Kent turns white as a ghost and is speechless and all his energy is drained from his body. Near collapse, he has trouble standing and holds the railing. Tears fall from his cheeks.

"It could be yours Kent."

"No it's not, and you know it."

She seems helpless.

"What should I do?"

"It is your baby, I can't advise you."

"Should I get an abortion?"

"I can't advise you. Please, it is too much for me.

Let's get out of this glass hallway. Call me. All of our dreams are smashed. You are the very air I breathe. My life is over."

She leaves crying in one direction and Kent leaves visibly shaken in the other holding the railing the entire way.

# CHAPTER XI

# THE SHRINK

That afternoon at the Psychiatrists Office.

"Thank you Doctor for seeing me without an appointment. I am at the very bottom now. It can not get any worse."

"Tell me Kent, what happened?

Kent breaks down in tears and tells the story of their commitment to each other crashing down by her pregnancy. The Doctor looking at Kent over his spectacles attentively inquires, "That is a sad story. What do you propose to do about it?"

"I have to give her up. I don't want to but I have to. I have to pick myself up off the floor and start over.

The pain is far beyond what I can endure I have to get my life in order. I have to meet new people. She was my life. Now I have nothing."

"How do you feel about your wife?"

"I don't love her. I have to eventually leave her."

"I am glad you came today, you are making progress."

"What does that mean, am I crazy?"

"No, you have what we call a character disorder, that's all." "You have been fighting your own character within yourself."

"Can you cure me?"

"No. You have to cure yourself. My role is to guide you through the questioning process so that you find your own answers. "Today for example, you have already made up your mind that it will eventually become necessary to leave your wife. Are you a Religious person?"

"Yes. I was brought up Catholic?"

"Catholics of course do not believe in divorce."

"I guess I will give up being a Catholic."

"You won't feel guilty?"

"I guess I will have to get over it. Guilt has been my biggest problem hasn't it."

"And your parents?"

"I guess I will have to grow up and not await my parents' judgments either."

"You love them dearly, they may surprise you. That's enough for today. You are at the bottom, there is only one way for you to go now and that is up. So pick yourself up and start over. I will be there to help."

*The Dead Oak Protects*
*Oil on Canvas, Impressionism*

# CHAPTER XII

# ART

Weeks later Kent is enrolled in an evening art class. He makes no effort to see Kim who quit her job three weeks after she found she was pregnant. He enjoys his new job, and has learned to relax with oil painting at night. Some forty year old women at the art studio taking the course are admiring one of Kent's paintings from the night before.

"What a romantic painting." commented one woman.

"It is so impressionistic," offered another.

"Crazy Kent" the art teacher responds. "I told him the woman in the daisies on the hilltop should have a long flowing dress, to be more romantic. No, he insists on a mini-skirt. He is a crazy painter. You will all like him, he has a mind of his own. All of his work comes out of his head. He copies nothing."

"Is this also his work?" asks another student.

"Yes," says the teacher. He calls it "Interlude".

"I even marvel at that one. All the light in the painting comes from the radio or a crack in the door across the room."

"Brilliant idea." comments a student.

The art teacher points to the radio in the painting and remarks, "I told him to get rid of the radio and use a candle, it would be more romantic."

"Your student Kent is a romantic, you can't tell him anything. That painting is so real, it is perfection in realism."

"It seems he painted this one with a palate knife?" asks a student.

"Yes", the teacher responds, it is rough but he makes his point."

*Interlude*
*Realism in the Degas Style*
*Oil on Canvas, using Palate Knife*

"I sure would like to meet him."

"Here he comes now." The teacher says. "He is early for the next class and he has no idea that the earlier classes critique and admire his paintings."

"Look at the size and unusual shape of the canvas he is carrying it has got to be 6 feet by two feet.

"Crazy Kent" the art teacher exclaims, "What are you going to do with such an unusual canvas, a wide picture of the Burlington Harbor?"

"Hi Ladies, no, you have it wrong." He turns the canvas the other way 2 feet wide and 6 feet high. "I'm gonna paint sunflowers as they are growing in a two foot patch of land I have."

The Art Teacher shrugs her shoulders with her arms outstretched; "Good idea, Crazy Kent. You entertain all of us."

He sets the canvas on the easel and sketches with charcoal the outline of his sunflowers. The women Ohh and Ahh.

*Sunflowers*
*Oil on Canvas*

"Kent, do you mind if I show the class your Surrealistic painting called State of My Mind."

Sure, go ahead.

The art teacher leaves the room and comes pack with the surrealistic painting and set it on an easel. The class is stunned.

One student asks, "That looks like the Bridge over the Winooski River, near St. Michael's College, is it?"

"Yes, good guess, says Kent.

Another student asks, "Why is there a painting within the painting, quite an unusual concept?

"It is my favorite painting called Absinthe by Edgar Degas."

Still another student asks, "Why is the man upside down at his desk?"

"The artist is disoriented, replies Kent, he surrounds himself with meaningful objects in an effort to right himself.

A woman asks, "Two cupcakes with candles indicate to me the involvement of a woman, am I close in my interpretation?"

"Right on! Yes."

The woman continues, "Leo is meaningful to you?"

"Yes! You might remember I said, when disoriented, surround yourself with that which is important to you in an effort to right yourself, the cup itself is important to me, the fact that is says Leo is incidental, although I was born in August."

"The title disturbs me, "the teacher asks. Can you explain?"

"Sure. Many Surrealistic paintings that you have seen before are done under the influence of hallucinatory drugs that were the rage in Europe during the last century."

"Although I have never used hallucinatory drugs of any kind, personal sadness overcame me to the point of becoming melancholy and feeling sorry for myself. The title of this painting The State of My Mind is quite accurate because I was hanging on by a thread while painting it as my morality was out of balance."

"Painting it became therapeutic; it became a form of closure like traveling through a dark tunnel with your eye on the speck of light at the end."

"At the end of the tunnel, you walk out into the bright sunshine, no longer feeling sorry for yourself, no longer melancholy but strong like Leo."

The men start clapping and the women with tears in their eyes are clapping as well as each of them can relate to their own life in this painting.

Even the teacher is smiling.

She says: "Thank you Kent," as the clapping continues.

*State of My Mind*
*Oil on canvas, brush*
*Surrealism, Dali Style*

# CHAPTER XIII

# ARCHITECTURE

COLCHESTER, VERMONT. 1972.

Kent has designed a contemporary home all glass and redwood and is talking to his builder. They are walking the lot. "Can you do it Bill?"

"We have to blast 500 feet and six feet down through solid rock to get you the water line from the street."

"Why so deep?"

"So the water won't freeze in winter. This site poses a lot of other problems as well. I will have to step the foundation to follow the contour of the rocky cliff. So it will be a four story house instead of three stories. Do you really need that art studio on the top with glass on four sides?"

"Yep. This is my dream house Bill. My own design as well. Each room is designed as the ideal for maximum function then independently room by room put together to form a house."

"I can save you a lot of money on the vertical siding if you use cedar."

"No Bill, it has to be heart Redwood. With nails that won't rust."

"The house is damn near all glass. I can save you money with metal sliders."

"Wooden sliders Bill, thermo pane, but wood framed, to be impervious to frost and condensation. I know you are trying to save me money Bill, but to me it is the ideal of what a home should be for a family of four."

The 4000 square foot "Dream House" is being built on a cliff overlooking Malletts Bay of Lake Champlain. The background of the Green Mountain Range with views of Mt. Mansfield and Camel's Hump only adds to the splendor of the view. Each morning Kent visits with his builder before going to work. His art lessons are over as architecture has now taken its place as Kent's new primary creative activity.

# CHAPTER XIV

# THE CURE

At work, Kent makes a conscious effort to meet new people. Each day he writes down in a book a name of someone he introduced himself to that he did not know before. His book already has 75 new names and he is feeling better about himself. He is trying to forget Kim and see if he can make his marriage work. The turning point came in September when he saw the play "Up with People" in Burlington. He came home with a big smile and could not help notice the three giant sunflowers in full bloom in the small patch of dirt between the stoop and the garage where he once cried his eyes out.

A week later. At the Psychiatrists Office.

Kent goes in and sits on the sofa and crosses his legs. "Hi Doc."

"This is your last visit, Kent."

"What do you mean, my last visit?"

"There is nothing more I can do to help you."

"But Doc, I need you."

"No you don't. Look at you now. You are an artist, an architect and a Corporate Executive on the Plant Manager's staff, you have made new friends. Your job takes you to all the major cities in the United States and many European cities as well. You are trying to repair your marriage and stick it out. There is nothing more I can do for you. You did it all yourself."

"I don't know Doc. I haven't been here even two months."

"When you first came here you sat in that hard wooden chair crying your eyes out. Now look at you, relaxed on the sofa as if to carry on an intellectual conversation with a friend."

"Well Doc, you are my friend. A father image, that I can bear my soul to."

"Remember, you cured yourself. I never told you to do anything except in our first meeting where I asked you to not make any decisions for awhile. You cured yourself. I didn't, and you made quick work of it by keeping busy with many outside activities. You will be forever stronger for this entire experience."

"Well thank you Doctor. I will never forget you helping me through this most difficult part of my life".

As Kent leaves the Doctors Office he thinks back to August when the sunflowers were ugly three foot stalks and now in full bloom at over six feet tall with the huge flower bending the stalk forward toward the sun.

# CHAPTER XV

# SERIAL MONOGAMY

Six months later.

The Dream Home is complete and the family moves in. "I don't know who you built this house for," says Darla, "you certainly did not build it for me."

"Well Darla, let us think of it as my expression of art in the form architecture. The ideas were inside me for a long time and I had to express myself."

"Like your paintings?"

"Yes! Every ounce of my being went into the design and construction."

"Our kids picked out each rock of the fireplace in Panton, Vermont."

"What are you going to do next?"

"We are going to Europe, Paris, Switzerland, Germany and Spain all paid for by the Company.

"You like your new job, don't you?"

"Yes, it is a wonderful job and I have a manager for whom I have a great respect."

"You had better never quit that job, I like all the security and the benefits."

A few days later Kent is just coming out of a downtown Burlington travel agency with his friend Fred.  He is carrying a bunch of travel folders on Paris and Switzerland.  Two women are approaching from the opposite direction.

"Kent.  You walked right by me."

"I'm sorry Kim, I didn't see you.   How are you doing?"

*Dream Home*
*Overlooking Lake Champlain and Green Mountain Range*

*Western Exposure*

*Southern Exposure*

*Panton Stone Fireplace*

*Front Entrance*

He looks at her big stomach and then her beautiful face and big bright eyes, her red hair is now cut short to her neck. Kim notices the travel folders.

"Kent, this is my sister Sharon."

"Hi Sharon, this is my friend Fred."

"Going to Europe, are you?"

"Yeah, the Company is sending me."

"I hope you have a better time than I had."

"I doubt it; I am going with my wife."

"Make a life for yourself Kent. I don't love Frank. I am going to be a mother, and all the love in my life will now be devoted to this child. You can call me sometimes."

"You are a beautiful woman Kim, pregnant as you are, and I wish you a happy life. I have learned so much about myself loving you and I will never make the same mistakes again."

"Like what?"

"We should have been married long ago, you gave me enough

chances. Divorce is finally and slowly becoming accepted in Vermont."

"You seem so much stronger now."

"I am. We have to go. Nice to meet you Sharon. She knows about us?"

"Yes. Good-bye."

The women continue their walk.

"That was quite a scene."

"I will always love her."

"I remember when you broke up. You transferred her to the lab and me as well."

"Dirty Doug was going to do you in, and he coveted her as his own secretary."

"You lost your job protecting us."

"I did what I thought was right at the time and now I have a better more exciting job."

"Kim quit the Company after a few weeks to stay home and prepare for her baby. How did you survive that?"

"I went to a Psychiatrist, once a week and worked hard to get my self esteem back."

"Are you going to leave Darla?"

"Eventually, yes. I love my children so it will be very difficult. But I will not make the same mistakes again. Do you realize how many times Kim said marry me now, and I didn't? Oh, so many times. Well, if I ever fall in love again, I will do it. I will not let the woman I love down as I have done twice now."

Fred explains that while working in Kent's department he always liked Kim and never suspected that there was anything going on between Kent and Kim.

"You are quite the Don Quixote, a hopeless romantic. I have an idea for you."

"What's that, Fred?"

"I have often thought of a way to live without guilt. I don't want one night stands with a woman any more than you do. I want a marriage before God like you had with Kim. So beautiful."

"That's what I want too Fred, but I have not found anyone that I could love like Kim."

"Well you first have to define it, I call it," "Serial Monogamy".

"Monogamy? Doesn't that mean only one woman?"

"Actually it means one partner. It is a good philosophy for women as well."

"Of course."

"However, in your case it means one woman at a time. You love them until it is over which might last many years, and never cheat on the woman you are with. You therefore live without feelings of guilt."

"Then what?"

"When it is over, it is over. You move on to find another woman to love."

"I get it. Serial Monogamy. It actually fits my poem that I wrote in the late sixties on the Purpose of Life. With Serial Monogamy you are always in love. Now all I have to do is find a woman that I can fall in love with."

"You will Kent, because you are the most resourceful person I know and someday you can write the Saga of Kent for others to learn how you spent your entire life in love. The poem you wrote is your destiny."

# CHAPTER XVI

# EUROPE

Darla and Kent are walking along the Champs de Elissey in Paris.

"A beautiful city Kent. What do you like best so far?"

"It was a thrill for me to see my favorite painting. I was taken aback just walking into a room and see L'Absinthe, the original painting by Degas at Jeu de Paume. The painting is much larger than the copy we have at home and I was captivated by his genius."

"What else, Kent?

"I like the way the Parisians kiss is public. I like that. Truly this is the city of love." Thinking to himself, "I will never come to Paris again unless I am with someone I love."

"How about you Darla?"

"I like the crepes and the pomme frits for sale by vendors on the street corners."

"We have had a good week here, tomorrow we leave for Zurich where we rent a car and drive to Grindenwald and Jungfrau, way up high in the Alps."

Days later on the sleeping car on a train from Frankfort to Hannover, Germany.

Darla is cranky, complaining about our first class accommodations on this wonderful European railroad experience. Kent refuses to let Darla get him more upset and tries to calm himself down and mutters to himself. "I have to leave this woman. We are just not compatible. The first two days on our trip to Hawaii she did the same thing and complained incessantly." Kent rolls over and looks out the window in the roomette watching the German Countryside go by and falls asleep.

Days Later on the Beach in Torremalinos Spain.
Darla and Kent sitting on a blanket in the sun and are observing various people on the beach.

"Kent! Look at the old guy with the young girl."

"What's wrong with that?"

"You know, he must be in his sixty's and she about 18."

"Yes. It is unusual. But I came here to see the unusual. It was Michener's Book, The Drifters that got me interested in visiting this place."

"Look, she is getting up and going into the water."

Kent gets up off the blanket.

"I'm gonna go talk to that guy, okay Darla?'

"Let me know what he says."

Kent walks over to the man in his sixties.

"She sure is beautiful."

"Yes, she makes me happy, have a seat if you like."

Kent sits on the beach chair. "Please forgive my questioning, but I need to know some of what you know to plan for my own future."

"Ha! I'll do what I can," says the man, "Fire away."

"How old are you?"

"Sixty three," the man volunteers.

"How do you attract such a young and beautiful woman?"

"It's easy", the man says. "Woman are not only into looks. Lots of women seek a worldly man."

"Tell me more. I am gonna be your age someday. I need to know."

"I speak seven languages which totally amaze women. That is really not so hard to do because if you know French then Italian and Spanish are so similar. I also speak German, Dutch, Hungarian and English."

"Wow!" says Kent.

"I am well traveled and read books. Women get tired of one night stands with people their own age. Some women seek the comfort of wisdom and a relationship with a man that can expand their horizons. They admire your brain and your life experiences."

"Are you wealthy?"

"In money no. In knowledge, yes."

"How long have you been with this young lady?"

"Almost a year."

"Here comes your little mermaid out of the sea. I will leave you to the joy of her love and I thank you sincerely for sharing your discoveries with me. I think I already knew some of what you told me, but I never heard anyone actually say it. Thank you, Thank you."

Kent gets up and walks away as his mentor smiles.

Kent is now back at work in Burlington, Vermont.

"How was your trip, Kent?"

"Great Al. A life experience I will never forget. Thanks for sending me."

"Your telegrams to me from Europe on computer memory failures were quite informative. The Bank in Solothurn, Switzerland putting fertilizer on their roof garden which they water every day was especially humorous. What I would like you to do now is go to any city that is having computer memory failures and find out why, like you did in Switzerland."

"Thanks, Al that is what makes this job fun. My next trip takes me to Minneapolis, Kansas City, Dallas, New Orleans and Tampa before I return."

"One thing I want you to include in your report."

"What?

Al sings, "Everything is up to date in Kansas City."

"They have gone about as far as they can go"

Ha. Ha. Ha. .They are both laughing.

# CHAPTER XVII

# SAILING

A quiet evening in The Dream Home.
"What are you reading, Kent?"
"A book on retirement."
"You're still in your thirties, don't you think it is a little early?"
"No Darla. It says here, people die in retirement early because they don't have a hobby to keep them busy. They should start a hobby that makes money in retirement."
"Well, you do oil paintings."
"I really need a hobby that makes me grow that can make some money in retirement. Do you remember when we were first married and lived in New Jersey and I showed you a sailboat that could sleep four?"
"Yes, I remember," says Darla.
"At that time you really had no interest and suggested that we wait until we have our house."
"Yes.'
"Well we have owned three houses since then and I don't think I will ever want one nicer than this one. So now it is time for the

sailboat, unless of course there is something that you want that I haven't bought for you yet."

"No. I don't think so," says Darla. "I won't sail on it."

"Well the kids will love it. Look how many times we have taken them camping in tents at Maine, Vermont, New Hampshire and Cape Cod Campsites. Now I can take them for a weekend cruise."

"You don't know how to sail do you?"

"No, but I will in six weeks, I just enrolled in sailing lessons at Fisher's Landing in Charlotte.

"What's in the bag? Kent."

"Well I want to buy that sailboat that I always wanted. So you have to start someplace."

He opens the bag.

"Voila! Boat shoes."

"When do you start lessons?"

"Tomorrow, after work. Two nights a week for six weeks. I will be done by July 15th. Would you like to take lessons with me?

"No. You go, maybe you can teach me."

In mid July Kent's first boat is delivered, a 24 foot Sloop which sleeps four comfortably. The kids loved it but Darla refused to go for a sail. She claimed she was afraid when it heeled over.

Six months later while on winter vacation in Tortola, British Virgin Islands.

Darla and Kent are sitting at lunch having pina coladas, when a young couple comes in and can't find a table.

"Join us if you like, suggests Kent."

"Thank you, I'm Mary Gotthardt and this is my husband Bob."

"Hi, this is my wife Darla and my name is Kent."

A Waitress comes over and takes their order.

"What brings you to Tortola?" inquires Mary.

My company sent me on a business trip to St. Croix, so we

decided to take and extra week and spend it here and visit St. John and St. Thomas. I think I made a mistake though.

"How?"

"I had no idea Tortola would be this beautiful or this Long Bay Resort so fantastic. I will hate to go to St. Thomas after this."

Bob says, "How long can you stay here with us?"

"Five more days here then two days in St.Thomas. What do you do for work Bob?"

"I really don't have to work, but I am trained as an architect. Mary works. She is a ballerina for the City Ballet Co. in New York.

"Wow. Pretty good Mary. How did you do that?"

"You just put your mind to it Darla. I was a high paid advertising executive on Madison Avenue. At night I took ballet lessons and finally quit to do what I wanted to do with my life."

"All we have is our life span, you might as well do with it that which you enjoy most," says Kent.

"Kent, do you like your job."

"Yes this year I do Mary, I have a great boss and a great job, but that won't last forever."

"Why do you say that?"

"I have already been with the Company 11 years. Only two years were rewarding and fantastic the other nine years were a waste of my life."

"What would you like to do?"

"Establish my own business in Yacht Sales."

"You are a sailor?" Bob asks.

"Yes, I had a 24 foot sloop last summer which I sold and have on order a 29 footer which will be delivered to the Montreal Boat Show next month where I will have it on display."

"So, you are already in business?" remarks Bob.

"At his point it is only a sideline for retirement."

Mary points out to sea: "Look at all those sailboats here pulling into the coves. Next year I would like to come here again and charter a boat. Kent, will you teach us how to sail?

"I would love to. Tortola is a sailors Paradise."

The last day on the beach in Tortola.

Bob, Mary, Darla and Kent have been inseparable all week. Bob is scuba diving with his mask nearby and Darla is getting four pina coladas. Kent and Mary are sitting together on the beach.

"Will you really come back next winter and charter a boat with us and teach us to sail?

"Of course. In fact I will teach you to sail on Lake Champlain. You and Bob can visit Vermont next summer and we will put you up for as long as you like."

"Oh! That would be great."

"Bob as an architect would like our house, as I designed it myself and it is like no other house. It is contemporary and all glass and redwood on a cliff overlooking Lake Champlain."

"Bob would like that."

Darla approaches with a tray of pina coladas.

"Here are your drinks."

"Thanks Darla" says Mary.

"I just invited Bob and Mary to Vermont next summer."

"That's great Kent."

"Come visit us too, we have a house on Long Island which has been photographed for one of the House Beautiful type Magazines, and an apartment in Greenwich Village which we use every day when I go to work."

# CHAPTER XVIII

# THE BALLERINA

Back at work in Al's Office.

"You asked to see me Al?"

"Well Kent, all good things must come to an end. Our job is complete here. We solved the computer failure problem worldwide. A job well done. I start a new senior level management job on Monday."

"Congratulations Al."

"Thank you Kent. Now what would you like to do?"

"I would like to get back into management in the Lab, not manufacturing."

"I will do what I can, in the meantime will you be my staff assistant in my new job?

"Of course, thanks for asking, I'll even make sure everything is still up to date in Kansas City."

"Ha. Ha. Did you visit all those fancy restaurants we used to talk about on all those trips?"

"Oh yes, I made each trip a gourmet experience. I visited the best restaurants in each city.  What great jobs we had Al.  I hate to see it end."

"Yeah me too."  Smiling as if reliving the restaurant experiences.

"They will move our furniture over the weekend Kent."

"OK, I'll be ready."


In Kent's new office a few weeks later.  The phone rings.

"Hello, Kent here."

"It's me."

"Hi, mother, how's the kid."

"Yeah, rub it in.  I love my child but I miss you a lot. Thanks for the Dr. Spock book.  Have you met anyone yet?"

"Well yes.  I met a ballerina, who is very beautiful, and she thinks like I do but she is married to a wealthy guy, so it would be futile to get involved."

"I know you can't go on like this.  You have to get involved.  You have so much to give a woman."

"I tried, but I have no feelings any more.  I have been with two women since we were together.  One of them you know, Barbara Collins."

"God, Kent.  She is the best looking Secretary in the entire company.  When did you do that?

"Just after you left.  I was trying to rebuild my self esteem."

"She is very beautiful, what happened?"

"You know how we used to talk for hours after we made love?"

"Yeah."

"Well, she just wanted to stay naked under the covers and watch television."

"Ha, Ha, Kent.  I spoiled you didn't I?"

"You sure did."

"What about the other one?"

"She is Asian and very intelligent."

"Come on, tell me."

"Okay. She is exotic and beautiful with long thick straight black hair way down past her ass."

"You know I cut my long red hair and now you are just trying to hurt my feelings?

"No. it's true. She was born in the Seychelles Islands and is part black and mostly Chinese. It didn't last more then a few months as she was married. She has a job in Cancer Research."

"You must have been horny."

"I probably was. You reach a point where you would rather have no one until you find the perfect right one. You are still the right one for me Kim."

"I know it, but you have to find someone. I want you to be happy."

"I am going to Montreal for ten days on Feb. 20th for the Montreal Boat Show. I will be staying at a fancy hotel and I want you to come with me. Bring the kid or get a sitter but come and we will be happy again."

"Oh. How I want that. Let me dream and think about it."

"We will be alone in the city where no one knows you.
We can do all the gourmet restaurants."

The next day Al walks into Kent's Office.

"Kent, did you hear what happened this morning?"

"No. What?"

"Ray Allen, 35 year's old found dead across his desk when fellow employees found him this morning."

"Heart attack?"

"That's what they think. They removed the body a few minutes ago. He must have been dead since working late last night."

"Makes you think, about what we are doing with our lives. Can we make our mark in life before that happens to us?"

"I hope so. That was the bad news, now do you want the good news?"

"Yeah."

"You have been promoted to Manager of Laboratory Design Systems Department. You start Monday with a new Department with eight employees."

"Thanks Al. You have been my mentor in a crisis time of my life and I will never forget it. We sure had fun together didn't we?

"Yeah. Good luck on your new job Kent.

Al shakes hands with Kent and leaves the office, just as Fred stops by: "Hi Kent."

"Hi Fred, have a seat."

"How did the boat show go?"

"I sold a few boats. My business is growing."

"Did Kim meet you in Montreal?"

"No she just dreamed about it. She couldn't get away."

"You must have met some beautiful French women."

"Ha, Fred. Over choice, there are too many to choose from, but I found just one, a beautiful redhead, Claire, she owns a dress shop."

"Well, any luck?"

"No, she wants nothing to do with me. She knows I like her, so she ignores me."

"Maybe next year."

"Yeah".

The following Summer on Malletts Bay, Lake Champlain. Mary and Bob are Visiting Vermont. Kent takes them out on his friend Duncan's sailboat and shows them the basics of sailing. The next morning Mary and Kent go to the store, on the way home they stop at Kent's Yacht Sales Office and Kent shows her around.

"Kent this is incredible! And it is only your side business.

"The way it is going it will be full time shortly because the yacht business is booming right now."

"How is your great job, do you like it? I remember you saying you only had two good years out of eleven."

"Well now it is three out of twelve. I am preparing to quit like you did on Madison Avenue as my definition of success is happiness. Money is not the answer."

"What does Darla think about that?"

"She is violently against it. She likes the financial security that the mother company provides. She wants no change in the status quo."

"So what will you do?"

"When the time is right I will leave both Darla and the Company."

"I could tell in Tortola you didn't love her."

"How?"

"The way you look at me, you see my soul."

"Yes, but I also see you will never leave the wealthy security Bob provides. I have to be very careful not to get hurt again. I was in love with a married woman and it almost destroyed me. No more married women for me. I do however admire your conviction to live the life of your dreams as a ballerina.

"We had better get back Kent, they are waiting for us.

# CHAPTER XIX

# TORTOLA

The following January they are back in Tortola, BVI Duncan and his wife Marge from Vermont joins the group as the three couples set sail on a 41 foot Ketch fully provisioned. Kent, Darla, Bob, Mary, Duncan and his wife Marge are quite excited as they leave Roadtown Harbor. Kent is at the wheel.

"Sail Ho, says Bob at the bow."

Mary smiles and is thinking out loud, "Incredible!"

"How about a beer Duncan?"

"Sure Kent, I will get you one."

"Hor's d' oeuvres anyone?" as Darla serves from a tray.

"I wonder how much snow they have in Vermont?" teases Marge.

"Ha. I don't miss it," says Darla.

Mary asks, "Each morning on land, I need to spend a half an hour stretching. I hope that is all right?"

Bob explains, "Yeah, she does her stretching routines. If she were to miss a day it takes many days to recover for ballet."

Kent jokingly explains, "We will call it part of our entertainment.

We all get to see some ballet while on vacation. Hey Mary, I always wondered? When a guy holds you up in the air by your 'you know what', what goes through your mind?"

"Ha! I think gay and that's the end of it. He is like a strong woman holding me up."

"You really love ballet don't you?" asks Kent.

"Oh yes. It is my life now. When I am too old to dance, I will become a teacher for the Ballet Co. Did you know I grew 2 inches."

"No," Darla suggests.

"Yes, from stretching. I used to be 5'4", two inches shorter, now I am 5' 6"."

A few days later the yacht enters Cane Garden Bay where it drops anchor for the evening. The next morning Kent rows Darla and Mary ashore for Mary's ballet exercises.

"What a workout, she really stretches," says Darla.

"Yes, it is quite something to see," as Kent proclaims, "I have to give her credit. She wanted it, she went after it, and now she is a ballerina."

*Kent at the wheel, leaving Roadtown Harbor, Tortola, BVI*

*Cane Garden Bay, Tortola, BVI*

*Cane Garden Bay, Tortola*

*Cane Garden Bay, Tortola*

*The three couples enjoy a brisk wind rounding
Tortola on an Out Island 41*

# CHAPTER XX

# MONTREAL

Weeks later at the Montreal Boat Show.

Kent is calling Kim from his hotel room. "Kim are you okay?

"I'm so sorry Kent that I can't be there with you. I really tried but I can't. I love you but this is impossible."

"I know, I understand."

"You make me feel so loved by always inviting me. You will find someone. I know you will."

He hangs up and goes downstairs and walks over to the fashion shop owner who ignored him last year.

"Hi Kent, I remember you from last year."

"Well Claire, you ignored me last year."

"I was involved, but not this year. Give me a pass to the show and I will come see your boats when I get off work.

"What time?"

"About nine."

At nine exactly Claire comes with her girlfriend to see the boats. The get on board an aft cabin 30' Yacht and when Kent shows her the double bed in the aft cabin she pushes him onto the bed and climbs on top of him and kisses him.

"Holy mackerel Claire, what's that for?"

"For coming back to see me this year."

"Well I am glad I did."

"I leave for my vacation in Acapulco tomorrow morning.

So you will still have to wait until I get back in ten days."

"I don't know if I can wait Claire, but I am sure you are worth the wait."

"Give me your card and I will visit you in Vermont when I get back. How far to Malletts Bay?"

"About an hour and a half."

"Okay bye, I'll visit you. I have to go. Kiss me again good bye."

They kiss.

# CHAPTER XXI

# THE FRENCH TEACHER

The next day in a cafeteria style restaurant.

Kent is sad and lonely thinking about the lost opportunity with Claire. He picks up some early lunch, pays at the register and walks with his tray into the dining room. There must be fifty tables, all of them empty except for a table with a young women having an early lunch. He walks over to a nearby table and sees that she is cute and in deep thought, then he intentionally changes direction and walks to her table.

"May I join you?"

The woman is totally surprised, but smiling.

"Well, Okay."

"Why should I eat alone when I can meet an attractive woman?"

"That's one I have never heard before. You must be American."

"How could you tell?"

"With all these empty tables ....."

"I understand. What's your name?"

"Lisa, and yours?"

"Kent, what do you do for work?"

"I am a French Teacher. And how about you?

"I sell yachts. I am here for the boat show."

"Are your boats here?"

"Yes. I will show you, after we eat if you like. Here is a pass to get in the show."

"I would like that."

Lisa spends the day with Kent at the show, they have dinner at a French Restaurant that evening with table side service and violins serenading them as they sip their wine. Later that evening in the hotel room Lisa is having an orgasm that has her completely broken down into tears.

"Ohh. Ohh. Ohh. I loved it. I needed that so much."

"It was good Lisa, but why are you crying?"

"I never had that happen to me before. I realize now I am ready for you. For many years since my divorce I was not ready for anyone. I know now I am ready, that's why I am crying. But you are married?"

"Not really. I live with my wife only as her abused husband and taken for granted provider. I do not love her."

"Can I work the Boat Show with you, if I take the week off from my job?" Lisa asks.

"Yes, of course."

"We can stay in my apartment tomorrow night. I will make you dinner and show you how we French women can cook."

"French cuisine, great!"

Lisa's Montreal Studio Apartment.

Just finishing dinner and making love.

"We have all week together Kent, but what happens after that?"

"I do not drive a car."

"The Greyhound Bus goes from Montreal to Burlington. Whenever you want to come down by bus, I will be waiting to pick you up in Burlington."

"Okay, that's a plan. Will you leave your wife?"

"Yes eventually. She is coming to the boat show with her girlfriends on Saturday Night. I'm not looking forward to it."

"Then I want you to stay here with me Saturday night.
Let her find your room empty."

"Ok. I will stay here with you Lisa."

Lisa and Kent were very happy together. She was a wonderful help selling yachts. The French people loved her and trusted her. She is petite, with dark hair and big eyes and a tiny nose, always smiling and bi-lingual. She seems the perfect match for an American in Montreal. The boat show ended and Darla with her girlfriend Nancy was embarrassed to find the hotel room empty on a Saturday night. Nancy gave her no comfort because she is known to gossip and the evidence of no husband not waiting for Darla was clear. Yacht Sales were so phenomenal as to be unbelievable.

Lisa visited a few weekends and stayed in a Mallets Bay Motel. With summer coming, Kent planned a second week sailing with Lisa on Lake Champlain. He told Darla he needed a rest from all the activity and wanted to sail alone again for still another week to get his head straight.

# CHAPTER XXII

# ROCINANTE

Kent's Office.

Kent is calling Kim. "Kim. Leave Frank, come with me now. I have a week on my boat alone. Please come, leave Frank. The time is now. Right now. Kent pauses: I will come and get you and your son. It is now, Kim. I am ready for you. Now!"

"Oh Kent, I want to, but you know I can't. I can't." She cries.

Lake Champlain on the Yacht Rocinante.

A 29 foot Sloop named for Don Quixote's horse, the transom painted by Kent's daughter Monica shows Don Quixote charging at windmills.

"I can't believe you have another free week Kent. The last one we had was our wonderful vacation."

"I can't believe it either, Lisa. This is our second week this summer that we have an entire week sailing."

"Where are we going?"

"The last time we did the northern part of the lake." "This time the entire lake to the South. Our first stop is Essex, New York."

"I will make you a cocktail."

"Thanks, Lisa."

They Kiss


It is evening on the sixth day in Orwell, Vermont.

The Yacht is docked and Lisa and Kent are just returning from dinner, when Kent spots Darla getting off his yacht.

"Oh, My God Lisa, it is Darla. Wait here, I will go up ahead and face the music."

"There you are Kent. "Where is she?" asks Darla. "I saw the Vee berth made up for two people and all her clothes hanging up in the locker."

"She is waiting over there Darla. Lisa, come here."

Lisa walks over to meet Darla.

"My God, she looks just like me," Darla says.

Darla starts crying.

"I am sorry you had to find out this way, but at least it is out in the open now. How did you get here? Here, sit down on this log."

Darla sits on the log and Lisa sits and Kent sits between them.

"Your brother in law Ed took me. We were all sitting around having a beer at his summer cottage, when he asked where you were. I told him you needed a rest and left on your boat for a week. He said, you don't believe that do you? I said I did. He laughed and said you have another woman. Watch he said, and picked up the telephone. He called Essex Marina. Has the Yacht Rocinante been there this week? They said yes. Was he alone? No he had a French girl. He called Westport Harbor, they said the same thing, then Basin Harbor Club on the Vermont side of the lake and Crown Point back in New York and finally here in Orwell, Vermont. It only took him 20 minutes to find your boat and an hour ride by car to get here. How could you do this to me?"

"I hope he is proud of himself. Where is he?"

"He is in the car waiting for me. Come home with me now Kent."

"No Darla. I'm sorry. I will be back tomorrow to pick up my things."

"Pick up your things?"

"It should be no surprise, I gave you a years warning to prepare for this. I told you last year that I would be gone within a year when you used vile language in front of the kids. I'm sorry, but it has to be."

She gets up crying and leaves.

"You did it Kent."

"It took me 14 years, but I did it."

"I love you."

"I love you too Lisa."

They make love like never before. The tension release that Kent feels for finally becoming an honest man is like no other feeling. The guilt trip is finally over.

At sunrise the next morning.

Rocinante casts off leaving the dock in Orwell, Vermont. The wind is brisk, and blowing from the South while we are heading North.

"This wind is a good omen Lisa."

"Yes. A heavy wind from the South."

"I'll bet we can make it all the way to Malletts Bay without a single tack."

"It's called a run isn't it Kent?"

"Yes, that's right. We will run before the wind and partially surf as the bow comes out of the water."

"Wow, we are already passing the Crown Point Bridge. At this rate we will be back in Malletts Bay by noon."

They sail up the Lake and enter Mallets Bay and finally come to the mooring at the Boat Club.

"Wait on board Lisa; I'll be back with my clothes."

"Promise you will be back. Don't let her talk you into staying."

"Don't worry, I'll be back."

He gets into his car and drives to the house. The scene in the Dream House is set. The children are sitting at the Kitchen table crying. Kent takes his clothes and puts them in the car. He takes his paintings off the walls and puts them in the car.

"Kent, you are not taking the paintings?"

"Yes, other then my clothes that's all I am taking. I'll even leave the Sunflower painting."

Monica now crying, "Daddy, you are not leaving us?"

Kent now crying too. "No Monica, I would never leave you or Stephen. I am leaving only your mother because it is time to straighten out my life. You both can ride your bikes or walk only two blocks to see your Dad every day at my Yacht Sales Office any time you want. I am there every day waiting just to see you."

"What about my bowling," asks Stephen?

"I will pick you up every Saturday morning and take you like I always do. Now give your Dad a kiss."

The two children hug their father as the father cries and pulls away tormented and leaves saying, "Remember, your Dad loves you both and I am only two blocks away any time you want to see me just ride your bikes, your Dad will be there waiting for you.

# CHAPTER XXIII

# FREEDOM

K ent rows out to the yacht to pick up Lisa. He is greeted with the biggest smile, and they row ashore in the dingy. "Come on, let's go ashore and have dinner and talk about our future."

"I thought you wouldn't come back."

"There is a time for everything. This is the time. I want you to quit your job in Montreal and move in with me."

"Where will we live?"

South Hero, a small community away from the gossips in the Champlain Islands.

"I will quit Monday; we can find an apartment and you can move what little furniture you have from Montreal.

Kent's Office at work, the telephone rings. "Kent here"

"It's me. Boy are you in trouble."

"I guess the word travels fast Kim."

"Darla, that bitch, called me to tell me you were fucking someone on your boat and that you left her. I think she knew about us all along and wanted to hurt me. Thank God, you called me first before you left on the trip or I would have told her off.

"Yes. I did call you first because I really wanted you."

"I knew what you were going through. You were afraid to fall in love with someone else. You wanted to give me one last chance, didn't you?"

"That's right Kim. I should have done this years ago when we were together. Divorce is so much more accepted in Vermont today than it was then."

"Darla did hurt me Kent, but thinking that it is my lack of courage not to be with you makes the hurt not so bad. I wish you and Lisa so much happiness."

She cries.

"How's the kid?"

"He is all I have now."

"Stay in touch Kim and thanks for letting me know that she knew about us all the time. It makes me feel like an abused husband that was manipulated for 14 years. I guess I am not so smart after all. I tried to protect her feelings all these years at a great cost to my own mental health, and she knew about us all the time. Just imagine the games she played to keep me prisoner of my own guilt."

"I know Kent, but you are free now."

Kent hangs up and the phone rings again.

"Kent here."

"Hi Kent, this is Carol, Darla called me last night in Florida to tell me what a rotten character you are."

"It's true, I am."

"No you are not, I want the best for you. Had you done that 6 years ago we would be married today."

"You were too young Carol."

"I was a mature 21 and you were ten years older and still growing up. I was ready for you. That was so nice of you to visit Dale and I when you had business in Tampa.

"The only reason I had business in Tampa was to visit you and Dale. I could go anywhere to investigate computer problems and I thought it would be nice to see how you guys were doing.

"Well we enjoyed your visit and we planted the tree you gave us to remember you by and it is growing fine, just like you are."

"You are just rubbing it in because I didn't get divorced 6 years ago. Hey, I will take the kids to Disney World this winter and stay on a yacht in Clearwater. I'll visit you and Dale then and introduce you to Lisa."

"Please do that and be happy. I wish you and Lisa the best, of all the people I know, you deserve to be happy the most. You have given me so much. See you when you visit."

Phone rings again.

"Hello, this is Kent."

"You are bad."

"Hi, Mary, she called you too?"

"She told me how bad you really are."

"I think she tells everyone whom she thinks I went to bed with."

"We never went to bed."

"Your fault not mine. You never offered."

"Ha! I think she is right, you are definitely bad. How's the new woman?"

"She is French, speaks the language to perfection, a wonderful help in my Yacht business."

"And the Yacht Business?"

"A Bonanza! I leave the company at lunch hour and go to my yacht sales office for an appointment and make between $6,000.00 and $10,000.00 in and hour. I can't imagine that I will last another year in Corporate America."

"You will quit?"

"That's right Mary; you had a lot to do with that decision so you should be the first to know. I will quit in my 14th year."

"I am so happy for you. Take care and visit us soon."

Kent hangs up as Fred walks into his office.

"Hi Fred, have a seat."

"Darla called my wife last night, you finally did it."

"I sure did. I will never get in that trap again. It is Serial Monogamy for me from now on."

"Right, stay with them as long as you love them, as soon as you don't, be honest with yourself and your spouse and move on."

"It is difficult with children, but without children it would be quite easy. In my separation agreement I am giving Darla $5,000 per month. A smart sale of the custom designed house to some Corporate Executives who have already looked at it would yield $500,000 and I intend to give $125,000 to each of my children and the $250,000 balance to Darla."

"You would give it all away?" Asked Fred.

"Sure, I earned it once; I hope to do it again, besides it is my kids we are talking about in this divorce. At least I will give my children a hard earned legacy for their education or for a start up business if they choose. It is not their fault that I can not love their mother who wants every dime I have."

No fault divorce is not yet the law in Vermont. By 1977 only nine states had No Fault Divorce, so it could be a long time coming.

# CHAPTER XXIV

# FATEFUL DECISIONS

The next Summer. A new 30 foot S2 Yacht is delivered and the transom is once again painted Rocinante. Kent is still at the company and Lisa is working in the yacht sales office. The phone rings with Lisa crying on the telephone.

"Kent here."

"There are cops here with guns drawn."

"What for?"

"They say they are from US Immigration and Border Patrol and want me to get in the car with them so they can deport me."

"Put the creep with the gun on the telephone."

"Sgt. Durkin. U.S. Border Patrol."

"Hey, Durkin. In this country you are innocent until proven guilty, so leave her the papers you are supposed to deliver, put your gun back in your holster and leave. Stop trying to scare innocent women because you are probably somebody's friend who is friends with my ex-wife who would just love it if Lisa were deported. Now put her back on the phone, unless you want to be charged with harassment and undue force."

"Howdid you do that, they are leaving?"

"Don't cry Lisa. I'll come to you now. Basically we have only ten days to beat your deportation."

Kent's Yacht Sales Office. Kent is calling Darla.

"Darla, I need a divorce in 10 days. I expect your cooperation."

"Ha! Fat chance! All my girlfriends say I can milk you dry."

"Well, milk me dry then. What do you want?"

"Everything! Every material thing that you own."

"You got it, so let's get on with it, the only stipulation I have is that 50% of the House goes equally to my two children. The other 50% goes to you, that way I have taken care of their college education or a start up business if they choose.

"You want nothing?"

"That's right. I want nothing material, only my freedom. Get your lawyer to draw it up with tomorrows date and I will sign it. Call me when it is ready."

"Okay."

Kent hangs up and dials his lawyer.

"Phil, I will have a divorce settlement signed and in your hands tomorrow. I need both an emergency divorce and emergency marriage and emergency passport, all within 8 days."

"Kent, you are crazy, this is Vermont, everything moves like molasses rolling uphill in the middle of winter.

"Do it Phil, you are the best."

"Okay, I will start the process and we will see how far we get."

Two days later at the Divorce Court, there is no argument because Kent has given Darla all his assets and the divorce is granted. The wedding invitations are sent out for the next weekend.

The day of the wedding arrives on three large yachts rafted together with about 50 people on board as Kent and Lisa are married. A Dingy is full of ice with about 70 bottles of champagne flowing. The honeymoon is to the Greek Islands, so Kent and Lisa stay in the

Holiday Inn near the airport overnight. The next morning Kent goes down to get a newspaper.

"My god look at that!" says Kent aloud.

He sees what looks like a picture of his wedding on the front page of the Sunday Newspaper in the coin machine. He is not sure as it is folded in half.

"Does anyone have change for a dollar?"

"I can break a dollar," offers a tourist.

Kent now having the correct change puts it into the machine and voila, it is his wedding on the front page of the Sunday paper showing the four yachts boats rafted together. You can actually see everyone on board with the preacher pronouncing the couple man and wife.

"Wait until Lisa sees this."

A wonderful wedding on board the yachts and a reception at the area's finest restaurant, the Newspaper Headlines and a honeymoon in the Greek Islands. Sounds like Camelot doesn't it? Lisa and Kent were together a total of six years with only two problems. Once in the fifth year Lisa said she wanted to leave and go back to Canada and live with her sister. Kent said he loved her but would not stand in her way. He packed up her sister's truck and she left.

That night Kent called his parents quite upset and said Lisa has left. Kent's mother said, she will be back. Four hours later at midnight, Lisa called and said she wanted to come back. So Kent, like a pack mule, went to Canada to pick up all her stuff the next morning with a rented truck.

# CHAPTER XXV

# UNUSUAL FRIENDSHIP

It was late September when Lisa furnishings were back in our house. just in time for the Oktoberfest in New Haven, Vermont. She likes beer so they went to enjoy the Oomph Pa Pa bands that were blaring away.

"How about a big beer, Lisa".

"Sure, I could sure go for one. Kent, there is a beautiful woman staring at you. It is Kim, I can tell.

"Where?"

"In the fifth row in the stands."

"My God it is Kim. How did you know?"

"Because she drinks you with her eyes."

"Come on I will introduce you. Hey Frank, how are you doing?"

"Hi Kent, long time no see."

"This is Lisa, she keeps me busy. I don't get out much any more."

"Ha. Ha. Now I understand."

"This is Kim, who was my secretary before we both left the company."

"Kent, talks about you a lot. He said you were the best secretary of his career. How's your family."

"I have three children now. After the first one the Doctor said I could not have any more children so I adopted a Peruvian girl, and then guess what? Surprise! I found out I was pregnant so now I have three children."

"After a few beers here Kent we are going to dinner in Middlebury to restaurant with an outdoor deck overlooking Otter Creek, would you like to join us?" Frank asks.

"Would you like that Lisa?"

"Sure I'd love to."

On the restaurant deck the two couples are sitting at a table having dinner.

"Did you finally retire," Kim asks Kent.

"I retired with 14 1/2 years of service. I really wanted to wait for 15 years but the boat business grew too fast. "

"I am so happy for you. You were not meant to be in an Engineering environment. You are an artist, educated in liberal arts and in the fine things in life. You always ment to be a free spirit and now you are one."

"Well I had three fantastic years out of 14, the other 11 years were a waste of time. Technology has such a short life span where art lasts forever."

"I see you succeeded in getting your Marina opened against all the opposition. It was in the newspapers every week for a year," says Frank.

"A real struggle Frank. It drained me financially but it is now open with 75 slips and 25 more on order."

Kim explained" "We see your TV ads on 60 Minutes every Sunday. The music to the theme of Rocky really gets your attention and is pretty clever."

"And your radio ads to Victory at Sea really make you want to buy a sailboat," ads Frank.

"You guys will have to come to North Hero, for a visit so I can show you around."

"We would like that." Kim smiles.

"How about yourself Frank. How's the construction business," inquires Kent.

"I have two homes under construction right now. It's a living. Kim is the one with the exciting job."

"What's that?"

"I'm on the Rescue Squad."

"Really?" says Lisa.

"Yes. Day or night, you never know when. I get a call, jump in the ambulance with the paramedics and go rescue someone and bring them to the hospital."

"I'm not surprised, Lisa. That's Kim's nature, to help people. It fits her pattern even to adopting the little Peruvian girl. You have so much love to give Kim and you never stop giving."

"Yeah, Kent I remember your poem in one word," and "What is Love?" "Giving!."

"Lisa and Kent in the car on the way home."

"I can see why you loved her Kent, she is so beautiful and so delicate.

"That part of my life is gone, Lisa."

"It is so nice that we can all be friends."

"You like her then?"

"Of course, I want her for a girl friend, she is so giving."

"They live an hour away from North Hero near Middlebury..

"We can visit occasionally."

"Imagine, Kim jumping into an ambulance in the middle of the night to go rescue somebody."

"She is a remarkable woman Kent."

# CHAPTER XXVI

# DILEMMA

In North Hero, Vermont, Kent and Lisa's home is called Five Oaks. The telephone rings and Lisa answers. "Hi Kim, It has been a few weeks since you called, what's up? Are you gonna visit us soon."

"Not for awhile, I haven't been feeling well lately. Is Kent home?"

"Yes, sure, I will put him on."

Lisa hands Kent the phone.

"Hi Kim, how are you doing?"

"I have cancer!"

Kent starts crying, Lisa is watching Kent's face and realizes there must be a tragedy and starts crying as well.

"No, not you!"

"Yes. It's lethal, the size of a quarter on my pancreas."

"Oh, God."

"Frank is taking me to a clinic in Tijuana, Mexico next week for treatments."

"Do you think they can cure it?"

"No, but they might slow it down. I just wanted to tell you myself and let both of you know not to call because I will be in Mexico."

"How long will you be gone?"

"A week to ten days. I have to go now, it was very hard for me to tell you this."

"I know. Our prayers are with you. Call when you get back." Kent hangs up.

"What is it?" Lisa asks.

"Cancer."

"Oh, No."

A year later at Five Oaks in North Hero. The telephone rings, Lisa answers.

"Hi Kim. How have you been?"

"Better. I have lost a lot of weight. I have changed my diet and am trying a holistic method of cure."

"Is it working?"

"It seems to, Lisa. The spot on my pancreas has been reduced, to the size of a dime rather than a quarter. But I am very weak, I get tired easy. I am going back to Tijuana again next month alone for treatment.

"Frank is not going with you?"

"No. There is nothing for him to do while I am getting treatment."

"Why don't you and Frank come and visit. I'll make dinner for you. Kent would love to see you."

"Sure we will come, but warn Kent that I get very tired and have no energy."

"How's this Saturday about two o'clock in the afternoon, and stay for dinner."

"Sure, thanks Lisa we look forward to it."

Saturday Morning at Five Oaks. North Hero. Vermont.

"Lisa, I have a favor to ask you."

"What's that Kent?"

"I don't want Kim to go to Mexico alone. Will you go with her for me?"

"That would cost you a lot of money."

"I don't care, I'll buy your tickets and give you a thousand dollars spending money so you can take her out. You will have credit cards as well. I just can't picture her alone on such a trip. She is so fragile."

"What a nice idea. I would love to go. I have never been to Mexico or San Diego for that matter either."

"You will love San Diego. Ask her today when you are alone with her. I will take Frank over to see the Marina and leave you two alone to talk."

"Okay, good idea. I hope she says I can go."

Big Red Murphy, the Irish Setter, barks: "They are here, Kent."

"Okay Lisa, get the door."

"Hi Lisa," says Kim, "what a beautiful lakefront home and your view is spectacular."

"Yeah, this is great," says Frank.

Kim pets the dog.

"Leave it to you Kent to have an Irish Setter, it fits your personality."

"How's that?"

"Irish Setters are free spirits, and so are you.
What's his name?"

"What did I used to jokingly call you?

"Big Red?"

"Well that's his name. Big Red Murphy of Five Oaks.
He is a pedigree; I had him since a pup at six weeks old."

"Ha. Ha. I saw the Five Oaks Sign as we entered your acreage and I noticed the giant oak trees."

"Yeah, there are five of them. Legend has it that the Indians used to meet the white man on this point of land protruding into Lake Champlain and the white man dropped acorns from his tobacco pouch causing these five oaks. Apparently the oak tree is not native to this area and they are very old.

"What an interesting story."

"How about some drinks?" Lisa asks.

"I'll have beer," says Frank.

"Kim?"

"I can't drink alcohol, but orange juice is fine."

"Is that the Marina I see on the opposite point?"

"Yes, it is only a mile across by water and six miles around by land. I can observe what is going on over there from here and remain in total privacy. Come on I will drive you over there and show you around.

"Would you like to come with us Kim?" asks Frank.

"No, I'll stay here with Lisa.

As Frank and Kent leave for the marina Kim walks around the house and notices for the first time Kent's paintings. She smiles as she sees "Interlude" the painting with the light coming from the old fashioned radio.

"These paintings all concern you Kim, do you recognize yourself."

"Of course Lisa, the radio is in our meeting place in Waterbury, Vermont. Kent must have told you everything about me."

"Yes Kim, he has, we have no secrets."

"I like that, and I like you Lisa for accepting me as a true friend."

"The radio scene is Kent's attempt at realism, while this one is his try at impressionism.

"Oh my God, it's the field of daisies. I still have that dress, but my hair is short." "Why am I alone?"

"It is symbolic Kim. You had left Kent so he is dead.

He is the dead tree. Look how the branches of the dead tree tries to protect you."

"How romantic, Lisa. The hilltop with daisies where we met so often. Kent is such a romantic, you are lucky to have found him."

"This painting is more the Dali style. You have become pregnant so that is Kent suspended in space upside down at his desk at work. Some good memories are also in the picture. The birthday cup cake with the candle on it. The coffee cup you gave him and the closed bridge over the Winooski River where you both tried to make things work out.

A few hours later dinner is served. The four of them are enjoying each others company.

"Frank, Lisa says she wants to go to Tijuana with me.

"There is nothing to do there Lisa."

"I would like to go with her if it is all right with you Frank."

"Sure it is Okay. What do think Kent?"

"It is fine with me. It's a chance for Lisa to see San Diego. She has never been out West."

"I would love you to come with me. Now I can look forward to the trip with Lisa."

A week later at Five Oaks, North Hero.

Lisa answers the phone. "Hi Kim."

"Frank's parents and my parents would like to meet you. Can you come and visit before our trip. They think it is so great that you are going with me."

"Sure, when do you want us?"

"How's next Saturday, at my house."

"Okay, we will be there."

# CHAPTER XXVII

# BETRAYAL

One week later, Malletts Bay Yacht Sales Office. Kent is calling his lawyer.

"Phil. I need you to prepare a document for Lisa to sign by tomorrow."

"What now?"

"A separation agreement, which gives her zero, absolutely nothing, zip, nada."

"She won't sign something like that."

"Yes she will, if you get it to me fast."

"What happened?"

"Well, about a year ago, she left me to go back to Montreal. A few hours later, she called and said it was a mistake and wanted to come back. So, I took her back. This time it is different. She left with one of my employees and moved in with him. So, when it's over it is over."

"I am sorry to hear that. I like Lisa."

"Everyone likes her. It is too bad, but it is over. I loved her dearly. Perhaps it is justifiable when you consider I left my first wife in pretty much the same way. That old cliché, "What goes around comes around," fits perfectly in this case."

"Are you gonna be okay?"

"I'm fine. I had a years warning so this time I am fine. Get me that paper by tomorrow. The last divorce I gave away all my material assets, because I felt guilty for what had become. This time I have no guilt whatsoever so let's make sure that she gets zero."

"I understand. You will need a witness present when she signs the paper."

"Okay. I'll have one of my employees present in the office."

The next day in the Malletts Bay Office. The phone rings.

"Kent here."

"Do you still want me to go to Mexico with Kim?"

"Yes."

"Do you have the Airline Tickets?"

"I have them here, pick them up any time."

"I'll stop by at four O'clock."

"All right."

4:00 p.m.

"Sam, I really appreciate you giving me all the details of what happened behind my back with Lisa. It made it very easy for me to get rid of her without emotion."

"I felt so bad Kent, but somebody had to tell you."

"She will be here in a few minutes and I will ask her to sign a separation agreement, you wait on the porch and when she is in the process of signing please come in the office so you can witness her signature."

"Okay Kent. Her car just pulled in the lot."

Sam goes out on the porch and sits in a rocking chair.

"Hi Sam, is Kent here?"

"He is inside, Lisa".

She goes in and Kent is at his desk.

"Do you have the plane tickets?"

"Yeah, right here."

Kent holds up the tickets.

"I have some papers for you to sign first."

"What are they?"

"A legal Separation Agreement. It makes our separation legal."

"I'll sign it, where do I sign."

Kent gives her a pen and points to the document.

"Right here and over here."

Sam is in the doorway observing.

"Sam, would you please come in here and witness this?"

"Sure, where do I sign Kent?"

"Below Lisa's signature and below my signature."

"Okay."

Sam signs and goes back on the porch.

"Kent, can I have the tickets now?"

"Sure. Here is $1,000.00 cash and a credit card. I will take you to the Airport; there is no need to let Kim know we are separated until you are both safely on the plane."

"What would you do if I refused to go?"

"Kim has to change planes in Chicago. I would go myself and surprise her in Chicago and we would both be on the same plane to San Diego."

"You have it all figured out don't you?"

"I would prefer that you go with her, but if you change your mind I won't let her travel alone."

"I'll go. I have never been to San Diego."

"Good. Here is your copy of our Separation Agreement."

Burlington Airport.

Frank kisses Kim good-bye, and Kim kisses Kent good bye and they get on the plane. Frank and Kent are waiting for the plane to take off.

"Thanks Kent for sending Lisa with her. I really appreciate it very much."

"I am happy to do it. You two are wonderful friends. By the way Lisa and I legally separated two days ago."

"I am so sorry to hear that. I can't be too surprised as I see it all the time."

"How's that?"

"I have built houses for couples who are separated by the time the house is finished. There are so many decisions to make on color and decoration that they argue so much that they split up."

"Ha. That is funny Frank. I remember Darla arguing when I built my house. She actually claimed I was building it for someone else and not for her. Well there they go."

The plane roars down the runway and takes off.

"Take care Kent. Stay in touch."

They shake hands and both leave.

# CHAPTER XXVIII

# THE ACCOUNTANT

The next morning Kent is making deposits at the bank to Susan the same pretty blond teller he always goes to.

"Hi Susan."

"Hi Kent, where is your wife?"

"I have no wife. We are legally separated."

"Does that mean, you can ask me out?"

"Sure, do you want to go out?"

"Yes."

"I have a problem. I will be in Annapolis for the next ten days."

"If I have waited this long Kent, I can wait another ten days. How about the Saturday Night when you return? I will meet you at the Danny's Club at 8:00."

"Sure, I look forward to it."

Midnight. Parking lot of Danny's Club.

Susan and Kent are walking toward Susan's car after a good time at the Night Club.

"Do you think my car will be safe here overnight?"

"Yeah, we will pick it up tomorrow."

"They walk over to Kent's yellow Corvette climb in and head for Five Oaks."

Five Oaks. Love Scene Kent and Susan.

"Kent, we are made for each other."

"How old are you Susan?"

"Twenty Three."

"My God, I am twenty years older than you. I remember a time I would not touch a women I loved because I was 11 years older then her.

"You are mine now," says Susan, "I am not going home to my apartment ever again. I will move in right away if you want me."

"Yes. I want you."

They kiss.

The Yacht Sales Office, Mallets Bay. About a week later.

The telephone rings and it is Lisa.

"Kent, I'm sorry, I want to come back."

"You can't, I am with someone else now."

"So fast. Who?"

"Susan, the pretty blond girl at the bank."

"She is too young for you."

"She is very intelligent, an accountant who graduated from Champlain College, Summa Cum Laude.

"You need someone that speaks French."

"Too late Lisa, She has already moved in."

"I don't even have my stuff out of the house yet, and she has the audacity to move in."

"I will leave the house empty tomorrow and you can get your stuff."

"I have to speak to you alone."

"Not gonna happen Lisa, I am already involved."

"Can I see you both then?"

"Okay, tomorrow night at the Sugarhouse at seven, we will be having dinner, you can join us."

Sugarhouse Restaurant at a corner table where Susan and Kent are having a cocktail when Lisa walks in and joins them.

"How was your trip," asks Kent.

"Good. San Diego is a beautiful place. Tijuana is depressing."

"How is Kim?"

"I don't think she will make it. She is too weak."

"What a tragedy."

"I am sorry to say this in front of you Susan, but I want to come back."

"He is mine now Lisa."

Lisa starts crying.

"Lisa, it is over. We had six wonderful years together and I loved you and was with no one else the entire time. I have moved on and am in love again. It is time for you to do the same."

"What am I going to do?"

"Be responsible for yourself and for your actions. I can't be responsible for you any longer."

"What about the car you bought me."

"I already called my banker, he agrees to transfer the remaining payments on the car to your name so you can keep the car."

"But you gave Darla everything in her divorce and you gave me nothing in ours."

"Darla is the mother of my children and I was the bad person. I lived a live of adultery and I was a very guilty person. I could not live with myself for what I had done, so I gave her everything."

"But you left me zero."

"That's right and I feel no guilt."

"I went to Five Oaks today and got my clothes out of the house and I saw the half burnt candles and champagne bottles all around the tub."

"We left in such a hurry this morning, I forgot about that," says Susan.

Lisa gets up crying and leaves.

Marina Internationale Office North Hero.

The phone rings and Darla is on the phone.

"Hi Kent, I heard about Lisa."

"How did you hear?"

"She applied for a job here at the High School as French Teacher."

"I hope she gets it, she will need something, the guy she is with doesn't even have a job."

"You can come back, you know."

"Thanks Darla, but I am already involved with Susan. Nice of you to offer."

Six months later Kim died. Kent was pretty upset and cried a lot. Susan knew the entire story and asked Kent if he was going to the funeral. Kent decided not to go because he knew he could not control his tears and it might embarrass both of their families. He would rather remember Kim the last day he saw her getting on the plane to San Diego.

Kent and Susan lived together for eight years until one day both people realized their relationship was over. It was an amicable breakup, neither party felt hurt and they remain good friends to this day.

# CHAPTER XXIX

# THE BACHELOR PAD

Kent moved out to a Lakefront Condo in Burlington and for the first time since age 23 Kent tried the bachelor lifestyle. "What a nice condo," says Fred, "good views of Lake Champlain, classical music on the stereo, a fireplace, a great bachelor pad. How is the single life?"

"A disaster Fred, I hate it. It was fun for six months but now I stay home and listen to classical music."

"What do you mean disaster?"

"Lot's of sex but no love. The women I meet all seem to be flakes. I have no trouble getting them in the sack, but when I wake up in morning I wonder why I even did it. I have not found a woman I could love, and to me that is so important."

"So what are you going to do?"

"For awhile I went out every night. I cut it down now to Friday nights only. I stopped looking completely and I stay home and listen to my stereo."

"Eventually Kent, you will find that perfect woman.

Shortly thereafter at a Burlington Night Club.

Kent sees a very well dressed beautiful, brunette woman talking to her girlfriend. He asks her to dance.

"What is your name?"

"Natalie. What's yours?"

"Kent."

"I have noticed you in Burlington often Kent, for the past few years."

"How's that?"

"You park at the Ethan Allen Club and walk down the hill and past my store for lunch almost every day."

"What store?"

"Jan Murphy's woman's fashions. I'm the manager."

"I knew you looked familiar. Last year at the sidewalk sale you smiled at me and said hi when I walked by."

"I remember Kent. You were too shy to talk to me."

"I was involved at the time."

"I have to go now, my girlfriend is waiting for me."

# CHAPTER XXX

# THE FASHION MODEL

Jan Murphy's Fashion Store.  Kent walks in and talks to Jan Murphy.

"Is Natalie here?"

"Natalie there is someone here for you," says Jan.

Smiling, "Hi Kent."

"Hi Natalie, I would like to see you again."

"Sure.  After work I have a cocktail with my girlfriend across the street.  Why don't you meet us at 5:30?"

"Okay.  I'll be there."

Local Bar.

Natalie and her girlfriend Gloria are sitting at a high table when Kent joins them.

"Hi Kent, this is Gloria."

"Glad to meet you Gloria."

"Hi Kent.  Natalie tells me you spend winters in California."

"Yeah, Gloria.  Vermont winters are to cold for an old fart like me.  I just moved my son out there in the sunshine and told him I would join him permanently as soon as I could."

"You don't look old, how old are you?" asks Gloria.

"Fifty three and the clock is ticking. How old are you ladies?"

"We are both thirty seven with the same ticking clock. You are not leaving for California soon are you?"

"Now that I have met you Natalie, I'm in no rush. It could take me a year."

"I would die for the California lifestyle, especially the food, "says Gloria.

"I'll tell you what. I have been told I am an excellent gourmet cook. Do you like fish?"

"Yes," says Gloria.

"Well, why don't you ladies come for dinner tomorrow night for some delicate California Cuisine?"

"What do you think Gloria?"

"That, Natalie, is an offer I can't refuse."

The two women show up at Kent's bachelor pad. They start with cocktails, classical music before the blazing fireplace. Natalie is making herself at home in the kitchen.

"Where do you keep the matches Kent so I can light the candles."

"In the drawer on the right."

"I think the fish is ready."

"OK, I'll serve it, says Kent."

"You relax and pour the wine, I'll serve it, says Natalie."

The three sit at the table. Gloria offers a toast. "To Chef Kent."

"This is delicious, says Natalie. How do you make it?"

"It is a joke how easy this meal is. Place three Filet of Red Snapper or Sole in a baking dish. Cover with salsa from a jar bake 15 minutes remove from oven and cover with Monterey Jack Cheese and bake for an additional five minutes. That's it."

"That's all. You would think it would take hours. The trick is the Salsa and the Monterey Jack."

*Bachelor Pad Overlooking Lake Champlain*

Days later at Jan Murphy's Fashion Store.

"Hi Natalie."

"Hi Kent, what a great time, we had at your place."

"Let's do it again, but this time just the two of us."

"Only if you let me cook."

"Sure, what are you going to cook?"

"Steak and Lobster."

"When?"

"After work tonight. I'll pick everything up and be over around six."

"Okay."

They kiss.

It wasn't until the second time Natelie cooked that Kent realized that she could cook only two meals. Lobster and Steak and, Ha, Ha, Steak and Lobster. It was Kent's former common-law wife Susan who told Kent that he was now with the most beautiful woman in all of Burlington. She said she always admired her because she looks exactly like the late Natalie Wood. Kent certainly agreed and eventually took up painting again and painted her portrait which hangs over the fireplace. Before working as Manager of Burlington's finest fashion shop Natalie was a fashion model graduating from John Robert Powers Modeling School in Ft. Lauderdale, Florida. Kent thinks back on their various disciplines of these women. A Mother, a Secretary, a French Teacher, an Accountant and now a Model and Fashion Store Manager. He considers himself very fortunate to have experienced their ideas and values all of which helped shape his own values.

*Natalie*

# CHAPTER XXXI

# SERIAL MONOGAMY EVALUATED

Twenty-one years later, Natalie and Kent are walking along the San Diego Embarcadero at sunset. Kent is 74 years old now and Natalie 57. They have spent a year in Burlington, Vermont together in a Lakefront Condo on Lake Champlain, then two years oceanfront in La Jolla, California with the waves breaking on the beach in front of their living room. After the ocean front we experienced mountain top living on La Jolla's Mt. Soledad with ocean views all the way to Mexico for another six years of their happy life and the remaining years in the vibrant and exciting downtown Marina District of San Diego.

Kent is reminiscing to Natalie as they hold hands.

"I am even older now than the man I met on the beach in Torremalinos, Spain. The advice he gave was not completely right, only partially right. It is true that some young women are attracted to worldly, educated men. If I wanted a woman in her twenties, it would be quite easy with my life experiences. However, where he wasn't completely right, is that it is wasted information as I have no desire for a woman in her twenties because I am happy and in love all these years with you Natalie.

"Kent, you worried so much about your children yet they turned out to be fine. How do you explain that?"

"My son was only eight when I left. It didn't bother him as much as it did my daughter. He visited me every day in my yacht sales office after school. I looked forward to him pulling up on his bike every day. My daughter was eleven, and didn't forgive me for the longest time. She was at an impressionable age when I left and very much under her mother's influence, so it took her quite a bit longer."

"Would it have been better if you stayed in the marriage for the kids?"

"No. I was a better father, only two blocks away in my Yacht Sales Office. I was a happy father, a content father, and a loving father who gave my children my undivided attention any time they wanted it. They saw no arguments between their mother and me, as I gave her all the material things I owned in the divorce. I left that marriage penniless. We did not argue over each pot and pan as most divorced couples do. The divorce was swift and without the slightest argument"

"You even gave away that beautiful glass contemporary home overlooking Lake Champlain?" Natalie retorted.

"I designed it as a home Natalie, but because I did not love Darla I learned to see it only a house. A home without love is only a house. Our home is a home wherever we are, because we have love."

"My son and I drove across the entire United States together with all his belongings so he could live near his Dad and when he got married he moved to a beautiful home in San Diego County.

My daughter lives with her husband in Vermont and has visited a few times and plans to visit again this year with my granddaughter.

Had I continued to stay in a bad marriage it would have served no purpose as Darla finally remarried and appears happy with her new husband. They both eventually sold the house for considerably less than I would have, because they really had no idea of its real value to an incoming corporate executive."

"Was Serial Monogamy the right course for you to take?" Natalie asks?

"Definitely, yes!"

"There were only two times in my life that I was continually unhappy. The first: the polygamous years of adultery where I had trouble accepting myself for what I had become. The second bad time was my only bachelor year when I was not in love until I found you. Serial Monogamy applies to women as well as to men, when you ask the question, why?"

"Why stay in a bad marriage?"

"Why not be in love all of your life?"

"Look at all the great times we have had together. We have traveled around the world together, visited all the continents and enjoyed more than 100 countries. We attended so many operas, symphonies and cultural events. We even smelled the roses in the many National Parks. Could we have had these good times if we were not in love?"

"I don't think so."

"I don't think so either, I love you Kent."

"Me too!"

So it seems time to take account of the value of Serial Monogamy as it applies to my past, my poem and to us.

DARLA – Married 16 years (polygamous)
KIM - Married before God 1 year.
LISA - Married 6 Years
SUSAN - Common Law Marriage 8 years.
NATALIE - Common Law Marriage 21 years

"I have no regrets, I would do it again, and after all I found you and have been monogamous and happy in love for 36 years. Kahlil Gibran in his poem The Prophet concerning love said it beautifully,"

"And think not that you can direct the course of love, for love if it finds you worthy, directs your course."

"So what do you think Natalie?  Am I wrong to follow my heart all these years?"

The beautiful Natalie, smiling responds:

"In One Word"

"What is the Purpose of Life?"

"LOVE!"

"What is Success?"

"HAPPINESS!"

"What is Happiness?"

"LOVE!"

"What is Love?"

"GIVING!"

Kent puts his arm around Natalie and they kiss as lovers do while the sun sets on San Diego Bay and the sky turns orange behind the purple clouds.

THE END

# THE AUTHOR

*John P. Roach Jr.*

Brought up in Glen Rock, NJ and attained a Liberal Arts Education through study of the Classics, Philosophy and Political Science at St. Michael's College in Vermont. He went on to take additional study on campus in his fields of interest at Seton Hall University, USC University of Southern California, Notre Dame University and Farleigh Dickinson University for Psychology, University of Vermont for Music and most recently Screenwriting at UCLA. Currently residing in San Diego, CA. The author has traveled the world and completed many screenplays and books on such diverse subjects as classical music, psychology, love, history, archeology, philosophy, opera, science, bigotry, politics and war.